Awesome Collection

by Mary Packard

and the Editors of Ripley Entertainment Inc.

illustrations by Leanne Franson

SCHOLASTIC INC.

New York   Toronto   London   Auckland   Sydney
Mexico City   New Delhi   Hong Kong   Buenos Aires

Developed by Nancy Hall, Inc.
Designed by R studio T
Photo research by Laura Miller

Awesome Animals, ISBN 0-439-42981-1, Copyright © 2003
by Ripley Entertainment Inc.

Bizarre Bugs, ISBN 0-439-41768-6, Copyright © 2002
by Ripley Entertainment Inc.

Blasts from the Past, ISBN 0-439-42980-3, Copyright © 2003
by Ripley Entertainment Inc.

World's Weirdest Gadgets, ISBN 0-439-41767-8, Copyright © 2002
by Ripley Entertainment Inc.

12 11 10 9 8 7 6 5 4 3 2 1   5 6 7 8 9/0
Printed in the U.S.A.   40

ISBN 0-681-15435-7

First compilation printing, February 2005

Awesome Animals

Contents

Introduction

Awesome Ideas

Robert Ripley published his first Believe It or Not! cartoon at the New York *Globe*. It was such a success that by 1922, his readership had reached 80 million. Many people wrote to Ripley, hoping he would use their ideas in one of his cartoons.

In 1937, a boy named Charles Schulz sent Ripley a cartoon about the ability of his dog

A HUNTING DOG THAT EATS *PINS, TACKS, SCREWS* AND *RAZOR BLADES* IS OWNED BY C.F. SCHULZ, St. Paul, Minn.

Sparky to eat pins, tacks, screws, and razor blades. Schulz would go on to publish a whole comic strip starring Sparky, called *Peanuts*. Sparky's fictional name? Snoopy, of course.

Sparky is just one of hundreds of animals whose stories can be found in the Ripley archives. When you consider that Ripley spent much of his life seeking out the remarkable, the bizarre, the mysterious, and the unexplainable, it's no wonder that so many animals have found their way into his Believe It or Not! cartoons.

What could be more bizarre than a miniature Seeing Eye pony wearing sneakers? Or more mysterious than dolphins appearing out of the blue to save a stranger from drowning? Or more unexplainable than a dog that goes and sits by the door to wait for its owner—not when she pulls into the driveway, but as soon as she leaves the hospital where she works? And, of course, the dog that rescued 92 passengers from a grounded ship during a storm certainly qualifies as remarkable.

You'll find lots of stories like these in *Awesome Animals*. You'll also get a chance to test your own animal smarts by answering the Creature Feature quizzes and the Brain Busters in each chapter. And don't forget to take the Pop Quiz at the end of the book. Finally, put your scores together to find out your Ripley's Rank!

Now, get ready to enter the amazing world of animals. You might just discover that they are a lot smarter, braver, and more unbelievable than you thought!

Believe It!®

Not long ago, scientists thought that only humans could use tools. But recent studies have shown that some animals not only use tools, they also behave like humans in other ways.

Smashed Eggs: The Egyptian vulture eats disgusting stuff like garbage and lion dung, but it also likes ostrich eggs. The shells, however, are too tough to peck open, and the eggs are much too big for vultures to pick up and drop onto a rock from the air. This clever bird grabs a stone with its beak, lifts it up, and throws it down hard at the egg. And it keeps doing it again and again until the egg cracks.

Creature Feature

When an elephant's trunk hangs down with the tip curled in, the elephant is probably saying it is . . .

a. happy.
b. bored.
c. frightened.
d. angry.

Cracking Up:

Chimpanzees love panda nuts. The trouble is, the nuts are almost impossible to crack open. Amazingly, some bands of African chimps have figured it out. The chimps carefully select heavy stones with naturally formed handles to use as hammers. Next, they set up nut-cracking stations, using tree roots or stumps to pound the nuts open on. Finally,

they practice their technique over and over again— pound too lightly and the nut won't crack; pound too hard and the nut gets pulverized. It takes about seven years for a chimp to master the process, but once it does, it can open as many as 100 panda nuts a day.

Sew Cozy:

Tailorbirds punch holes around the edges of leaves with their beaks. Then they stitch the sides together with grass to make a cozy pocket— the perfect nest to raise their chicks in.

Creature Feature

While hunting for food among the sharp-edged coral reefs, porpoises often cover their tender noses with face masks they fashion out of . . .

a. sponges.
b. mud.
c. clamshells.
d. seaweed.

Toolin' Around:

Chimpanzees use tools to help them capture insect prey. They find twigs that are long and sturdy enough to poke into termite mounds. The termites scurry out, and the chimps scoop them into their mouths. There's nothing like a crunchy snack!

Shell Game: Abalone shells can be hard to break open. But that doesn't stop sea otters from getting inside them. While floating on its back, the otter sets a flat rock on its stomach. Then it bangs the abalone on the rock. The shell cracks open, and the otter dines on its favorite seafood.

Wireless: Workers at Blair Drummond Wildlife Park in Stirling, Scotland, got annoyed when they began getting prank calls—until they figured out who the culprit was. A chimpanzee named Chippy had swiped the chief game warden's

cell phone and, while his caregivers were sleeping, he pressed speed dial, waking them up in the middle of the night. It wasn't until he let out one of his signature screeches that his cover was blown. Now that his phone privileges have been suspended, Chippy is working on new ways to drive his caretakers bananas!

Tickled Pink: Rats are having fun at Ohio's Bowling Green State University psychology lab. With the help of ultrasonic devices, Jaak Panksepp discovered that rats make distinct chirping noises when they play with each other. When he tickled the rats on the back of the neck, the chirping noises increased. For Panksepp, who has been studying emotions for more than 20 years, this discovery was no laughing matter!

Counting on Isaac: Isaac is a golden retriever that can add, subtract, multiply, divide, and even do square roots. When Isaac was a pup, his owner, Gary Wimer, spent 20 minutes a day teaching him to count. The puppy loved his lessons and soon began astounding everyone who came into contact with him. All Wimer has to do is ask the little genius what the square root of 36 is, and Isaac will bark six times. He even helps Wimer's eight-year-old with his arithmetic. Imagine having a dog that can help you with your homework!

Creature Feature

Most rats will do anything to avoid becoming a cat snack. But once in a while, a rat will find itself irresistibly drawn to a cat because it . . .

a. wants to make friends.
b. wants to share the cat food.
c. is infected with *Toxoplasma gondii.*
d. is schizophrenic.

...I'll see you tomorrow!

Bird Brainiac: When Irene Pepperberg, a professor at the University of Arizona, says good night, she typically hears the reply, "Bye. I'm gonna go eat dinner. I'll see you tomorrow." Though the response is not unusual, the source is. It comes from Alex, an African gray parrot, Pepperberg's main research subject for more than 20 years. Alex has a 100-word vocabulary and can identify 50 different objects—not just by name, but also by how they are similar to one another. Pepperberg's study has proven that Alex is not merely "parroting" what he hears but is actually processing information.

A Beautiful Mind:

Koko, a lowland gorilla, has a vocabulary of more than 1,000 signs and understands 2,000 words of spoken English. A participant in the Gorilla Language Project, Koko has an IQ between 70 and 95. (One hundred is considered average for humans.) Koko is imaginative as well as smart. When playing with her dolls, she arranges their arms and hands in certain positions and pretends that they are signing, too!

Pulling Strings: Bernd Heinrich is a zoologist who specializes in studying ravens. One thing he's discovered is that they're very intelligent. Their results on the IQ tests he gives them are proof. Heinrich attaches a long string with a piece of food at the end to a high perch. To get to the food, a raven will have to repeat one step 30 times in a row. The bird has to lift up a length of string with one foot, then hold it down with the other foot while it pulls up a second length. It must repeat the process over and over again until it gets to the end of the string. Heinrich has found that most ravens can figure out how to do this within minutes.

Creature Feature

Sheep can tell which animals are other sheep . . .

a. when they are shown photos.
b. by the shape of their eyes.
c. through ESP (extrasensory perception).
d. even when blindfolded.

Screen Test:

Washington Zoo biologist Rob Shumaker is teaching words to orangutans. Azy, a 21-year-old male is his best student. Even Azy's mistakes show how smart he is. When presented with closed bags containing chopped fruit and asked to find the matching symbol on a computer screen, Azy picked a cup instead of a bag—a mistake that shows he is capable of organizing words into categories!

Little Squealer: When a New York City restaurant owner was murdered on July 12, 1942, his green parrot told police the name of the killer. The bird had been taught to identify patrons by name, so when the parrot kept repeating the same name over and over, the police knew they had their man!

Creature Feature

Ospreys, which are also called fish hawks, locate good places to fish by . . .

a. catching the scent of fish on the thermals that rise up from the sea.
b. watching the flight patterns of other birds.
c. following fishing boats.
d. listening for splashes as they fly over the water.

Something to Crow About: What does a crow do when it has too much to carry? One clever crow in Washington's Olympic Mountains was observed with this problem. On  the ground were several crackers that the crow wanted all for itself. Each time it picked one up and then opened its beak to get another, the first cracker fell out of its mouth. That's when the crow did some pretty awesome problem-solving. It propped the crackers very close together—like sliced bread—in the snow. Then it opened wide and grabbed all seven in its beak at once!

Name That Tune: Trainers at a German zoo taught a female elephant to identify several tunes. Though they  tried to stump her by varying speeds, changing rhythms, and using different instruments, the elephant still recognized every one. In another experiment, she was taught to match patterns on cards. Six hundred pairs of cards later, she got a perfect score—even after a year had passed!

Mathpanzee: Dr. Sally Boysen, director of the Primate Cognition Center of Ohio State University, is teaching chimpanzees about numbers. One day, she dropped three peaches in one box and three in another. Then she took out number cards and asked Sheba, one of the chimps, how many peaches were in the boxes. When Sheba pointed to six, Boysen was astounded. Though the chimp had been taught to recognize numbers and to put them in order, she had never been taught to count or add!

Piggin' Out: Professor Stanley Curtis at Pennsylvania State University has proved that pigs are extremely observant creatures with excellent memories. How? By teaching them to play video games. Using their snouts to control the joysticks, six pigs—Ebony, Ivory, Pork, Beans, Jekyll, and Hyde—started out by moving the cursor through simple mazes. Then they went on to more complex games where they had to match similar objects or hit a target that got smaller and smaller. Of course, the pigs were well motivated: Their efforts were instantly rewarded with M&Ms.

Putting Their Feet Down: Zoologists from Stanford University have discovered that elephants have a unique way of communicating over long distances. How do they do it? With a series of stomps that send vibrations rippling through the ground. The vibrations are picked up at the other end by the receiving elephants' toenails, then travel up their bones to the elephants' ears. Typical messages are warnings that danger is near and have been heeded by elephants as far as 20 miles away!

Creature Feature

Though no one noticed when King Henry III's pet parrot, whose wings were clipped, fell into the Thames River, it was saved because it . . .

a. squawked "boat."
b. knew how to doggy paddle.
c. squawked "help!"
d. wore a mini life preserver.

Cat Burglar: When citizens in Guelph, Ontario, Canada, started to notice that some of their things were missing, they suspected that a burglar was afoot. But what kind of bandit would steal gloves, shirts, shoes, toys, and even a
bag of potatoes? Amber Queen cracked the case when she found Moo, her 15-pound cat, trying to drag some of the missing items through her cat door. Moo hasn't reformed, but Queen makes every effort to return the loot by placing ads in the local newspaper and putting up lists of stolen items around town. Luckily for Moo, no one has tried to press charges—yet!

Scrambled Eggs: For years, scientists have known that the cuckoo lays its eggs in other birds' nests to avoid the wing-breaking work of raising its chicks. But they haven't been sure why the magpies are such willing foster mothers. Now they know that a cuckoo will fly by to check the nest and make sure that the magpie hasn't tossed the cuckoo egg out. If it has, the cuckoo will destroy the nest and all the magpie's eggs or chicks!

Cat Attack: Lions specialize in cooperative hunting. But who knew that they were smart enough to plan their strategy ahead of time? Dr. Donald Griffin, who studies animals in the wild, watched four female lions go after a wildebeest. To distract the herd, two of the lions deliberately placed themselves where the wildebeests could see them. The third lion crawled through the grass until she was midway between the lions and herd and crouched, unseen. The fourth lion charged from behind the herd, sending the animals running toward the hidden lion, who burst from cover and killed one of the wildebeests. All four lions shared in the kill!

Creature Feature

Darrel is a chimpanzee who can . . .

a. write his name.
b. play checkers.
c. win video games.
d. understand fractions.

Pop Singers:

Scientists eavesdropping on black-capped chickadees have discovered that the males of the species regularly have singing contests! Female chickadees are the judges. The male with the loudest, most aggressive-sounding song is the winner. His prize? He gets to mate with the most females. Scientists have proved this theory by genetically testing chicks for paternity. As expected, the best singers had fathered the most chicks!

By the Book: Danny Younger, a parakeet owned by Ella Hohenstein of St. Louis, Missouri, flew the coop. Four weeks later, the bird was returned home. Because the bird kept repeating his name, the people who found him decided to see if his last name was in the telephone book. Sure enough, they found an identical listing—which was for Hohenstein's grandson after whom the parakeet was named.

Creature Feature

Sparkie Williams, a parrot, knows 531 words and can . . .

a. perform a high-wire act.
b. play the flute.
c. recite eight nursery rhymes.
d. build castles with Lego toys.

Think Tanks: Scientists have always believed that invertebrates (animals without backbones) are at the bottom of the IQ scale, capable of little more than the most basic survival skills. Yet the octopuses at the Seattle Aquarium appeared to be playing—a behavior that requires a considerable amount of thinking! So marine biologists Roland Anderson and Jennifer Mather decided to place empty bottles in the octopuses' tanks and watch to see what they would do. "One blew the bottle back and forth against a water inlet, a little like bouncing a ball, and one blew the bottle around the tank," said Anderson. It looks like some invertebrates are smarter than people thought—except for the folks at the Ripley's Aquarium in South Carolina. One octopus there figured out how to open its tank, crawl out, and eat the fish in the next tank, then return to its own tank and close it, fooling everyone until it was finally caught in the act!

Mud-Packers: Work elephants in Myanmar have been known to stuff the bells around their necks with mud. Why? So that the bells won't ring when the elephants sneak out at night to steal the bananas they love to eat!

Creature Feature

Ken Allen, who lives at the San Diego Zoo, is . . .

a. an orangutan that regularly dismantles its cage.
b. a koala that picks the lock on its cage.
c. a gorilla that can turn off its electrified fence.
d. a lemur that can slip through the bars of its cage.

Brain Buster

It can be a real *beast* trying to tell the difference between fact and fiction—especially when the truth is so bizarre. Think you're up to the challenge?

Robert Ripley dedicated his life to seeking out the bizarre and unusual. But every unbelievable thing he recorded was known to be true. In the Brain Busters at the end of every chapter, you'll play Ripley's role—trying to verify the fantastic facts presented. Each Ripley's Brain Buster contains a group of four shocking statements. But of these so-called "facts," **one** is **fiction**. Will you **Believe It!** or **Not!**?

Wait—there's more! Following the Brain Busters are special bonus questions in which you'll try to solve one more "wildlife wonder." to see how you rate, flip to the end of the book for answer keys and a scorecard.

Human nature? Lots of animals have abilities similar to humans'. Three of the following examples are true and one is false. Can you spot the one bogus animal behavior?

a. When a beekeeper dies, his or her bees will often use their amazing navigational skills to find their keeper's grave and say "good-bye" to their old master.

Believe It!   **Not!**

b. All porcupines can float.

Believe It!   **Not!**

c. Despite its size, a black rhinoceros can outrun most human sprinters.

Believe It!   **Not!**

d. Piranhas will actually gather together for meals around rocks that they use like tables.

Believe It!   **Not!**

• •

BONUS QUESTION—WILDLIFE WONDER

A baby gray whale drinks a lot of milk! How much? Enough to fill more than 2,000 bottles a day.

Believe It!   **Not!**

Some jobs are so highly specialized that only a nonhuman can do them.

Photo Finish: In Fort Collins, Colorado, David Costlow, owner of a white-water rafting company, has solved one very vexing problem. Part of his service is providing customers with a photograph to remember their trip by. The trouble is,

because of the steep, winding canyon roads, it often takes longer to get the film developed than it does to complete the entire white-water adventure! So Costlow straps tiny backpacks to pigeons, who fly the film over the canyon to base camp so the pictures can be developed by the time the rafters return!

Creature Feature

Old Pete, who guards a flock of sheep at a prison farm in South America, is a . . .

a. 300-pound ostrich.
b. three-legged Old English sheepdog.
c. 500-pound gorilla.
d. seven-ton elephant.

Spitting Image:

After Michael Riding lost 20 sheep to coyotes in just one year, he decided to get them a bodyguard—one that was fierce, loyal, and protective. Enter Ping, a llama with all those

qualities and more. Coyotes hunt by separating one sheep from the rest. When Ping senses danger, he circles the flock to keep all of the sheep together. If one sheep begins to stray, Ping will spit and hiss to make it behave. In the five years that Ping's been on the job, Riding has lost no more than two sheep a year.

Scratch and Sniff:

Extremely active dogs don't necessarily make the best pets, but they do make terrific drug-detectors. Trained to patrol heavily trafficked areas such as airports, bus depots, and sports arenas, one dog can inspect up to 500 packages, suitcases, and backpacks in less than 30 minutes—a job that would take a person several days. In mailrooms and airports, dogs even have to jump on moving conveyor belts. During his career, Chopper, a 10-year veteran of the Customs Service, found more than 80 million dollars worth of smuggled drugs! Retired now, he lives a quiet life with his handler.

Making Scents: A trained bomb-sniffing dog can find very small amounts of explosives within minutes. Unlike drug-sniffing dogs, they have to stay very calm so they won't accidentally set off any explosives. In 1972, a Los Angeles-bound Boeing 707 turned around and returned to John F. Kennedy Airport after someone called in a bomb threat. Brandy, a German shepherd who worked with the local police department, was on the job. In short order, she located a bomb made of C-4, a powerful plastic explosive, inside a briefcase—just 12 minutes before it was set to go off.

Creature Feature

Teddy, a calico cat owned by Kathleen Calligan of Huntsville, Alabama, is . . .

a. an ordained minister.
b. the town mayor.
c. a school mascot.
d. a dogcatcher.

Techno Rat: Dr. Judy Reevis, an information technologist, wanted to hook up an old classroom to the Internet. The cramped space above the ceiling made it impossible for her to do the wiring herself, so she decided to train a rat to do the work. First, she tied a string around a rat named Ratty and attached the other end to a line  of cable. She then sent Ratty, who can pull up to 250 feet of cable at a time, through the ceiling to do his job. Dr. Reevis knocked on the ceiling to keep him moving in the right direction. To date, Ratty has wired ten schools.

Who's the Boss? Before it can be on the job full-time, a Seeing Eye dog has to learn how to take various paths around obstacles, judge heights so it can prevent its human from bumping into low overhead objects like branches and awnings, and understand commands such as left, right, stop, and forward. But, by far, the most important lesson a guide dog must learn is to disobey! Many dogs have saved their owners' life by refusing a command that would place them in the path of danger.

Top Dog: Allen Parton suffers from memory loss and partial paralysis sustained during the Gulf War. With the help of Canine Partners for Independence in Hampshire, England, Parton and Endal, his Labrador retriever, have developed a special sign  language. When Parton forgets the names of things, all he has to do is tap his head, touch his cheek, or rub his hands together, and Endal will fetch his hat, his razor, or his gloves, respectively. The dog can also help shop, withdraw money from an ATM (automated teller machine), and load and unload the washer and dryer!

Creature Feature

In the 1960s, mail was carried over the Dead Heart desert in Australia by . . .

a. a kangaroo with a pouch full of letters.
b. six dingoes pulling a cart.
c. camels pulling a car with no engine.
d. a pack of koalas.

Slow but Sure: Juan Solis of Bolivia was totally blind. Luckily, he had a smart four-legged friend to help him out—a giant tortoise who led Solis safely around town.

No Horsing Around:

Cuddles, a miniature horse just two feet tall, is the first guide horse for the blind in the United States. Cuddles's training by the Guide Horse Foundation was put to the test when she and her owner, Dan Shaw, passed through New York City on the way to her new home in Maine. Clad in tiny sneakers to keep her from slipping, Cuddles took the busy streets and noisy subways right in stride.

Dog-eared: What happens when an emergency vehicle comes screeching down the road behind a driver who is deaf? In the absence of a hearing human passenger, a specially trained dog seated next to a deaf driver is the perfect solution. The dog alerts its human by gently placing a paw on his or her leg. At home, the dog will nuzzle its owner awake and alert him or her to other sound signals, such as a doorbell, a crying baby, or a smoke alarm.

Speedy Delivery: Sending messages by pigeon dates back to ancient times. During World War II, radio and telegraph messages could be intercepted, so the United States used 56,000 of these swift birds, which can fly 70 miles per hour and cover 700 miles a day, to carry important communications from place to place.

Cap and Bone: Darcy James, a four-year-old German shepherd guide dog, graduated from Mississippi State University with her mistress, Barbara James. In recognition of the splendid job Darcy did leading Barbara from class to class, university officials awarded her special academic honors. Darcy, however, was much more interested in the doggy treats she also received as her reward.

Creature Feature

A building erected by monks in Compiègne, France, is called the Abbey of . . .

a. Bear Field, because a trained bear was used to clear the construction site.
b. Canine Comfort, because the monks trained dogs to provide aid to the residents of a leper colony.
c. Feline Friendship, because the monks had 150 cats to keep the abbey from being overrun by mice.
d. Canine Guidance, because the monks were blind and depended on Seeing Eye dogs to guide them.

Bright Idea: For some people who are paralyzed, capuchin monkeys serve as all-around lifelines. Trained by an organization called Helping Hands, a capuchin monkey will fetch an object that its owner points to with a laser light. The light, which is attached to a wheelchair, can be manipulated by a person's mouth. The monkey can turn pages of a book, open a refrigerator, pop the top of a prepared beverage and insert a straw, unwrap a sandwich, feed its owner, and even scratch an annoying itch!

Creature Feature

In 1917, as part of the World War I conservation effort, sheep were used to . . .

a. pull schoolchildren in carts to conserve fuel.
b. trim the White House lawn.
c. provide families with milk.
d. guard army camps at night.

Clean Sweep: An elephant owned by the Duke of Devonshire, England, was trained to wet down the walks of a park with a watering can and then sweep them with a broom.

Canine Delivery:

For a three-year period in the late 1800s, a German shepherd dog named Dorsey was the only mail carrier between the towns of Calico and Bismarck in California's Mojave Desert. Dorsey never once missed his regular schedule on the three-mile trip.

Deep Snout: Luise,
a 250-pound wild boar, has been trained by German police to root out hidden drugs that even dogs can't find. Her sense of smell is so acute that she can locate drugs buried under four feet of earth.

Monkey Business: Dore Schary was the production head of the MGM Studios from 1948 to 1956. But when he first started out as a young writer at Columbia Pictures, Schary worked on a jungle movie in which a monkey was paid more for one day of work than Schary received for a week.

Creature Feature

At the court of King Louis XVI, the entertainment often included . . .

a. trained poodles jumping through hoops of fire.
b. costumed parrots singing opera.
c. monkeys in tuxedos playing flutes.
d. pigs in pantaloons dancing to bagpipes.

Crazy creatures! Some animals have abilities that humans only dream of. Can you spot the one amazing animal fact that's incredibly untrue?

a. When the risk of attack is high, mallard ducks will sleep with one eye open and half of their brain "awake." They sleep normally when the risk is low.

Believe It!   **Not!**

b. A grizzly bear's nose knows! These big tough guys have such a powerful sense of smell that they can detect a human who is two miles away!

Believe It!   **Not!**

c. Not only can an owl see in the dark, it can also see behind itself by using the extra set of eyes in the back of its head.

Believe It!   **Not!**

d. An aardvark can dig its way through a termite mound (a feat in itself!). But even more impressive is its thick skin—which allows it to feel no pain, even when the termites start stinging!

Believe It!   **Not!**

BONUS QUESTION—WILDLIFE WONDER

Many lizards have a third eye in the back of their head, though in some species it is more developed than in others.

Believe It!   **Not!**

The connections formed between animals of different species can sometimes seem downright magical.

Milk Maid: When a stray cat broke its leg in a fight, Susan Trumblay took her to an animal hospital to recuperate, and took the cat's three-week-old kittens home. Trumblay thought she was going to have to feed the little ones formula with an eyedropper. But her female Pomeranian dog, who had never even had a litter of puppies, had other ideas. Amazingly, the little dog began to produce milk and nursed the kittens herself!

Creature Feature

A cat owned by A. W. Mitchell of Vancouver, British Columbia, nurtured . . .

a. six baby Canada geese.
b. 25 chicks.
c. three baby raccoons.
d. eight newborn rats.

Mistaken Identity:

Lisa Embree was in her backyard when she found an abandoned baby squirrel. Embree tried to feed the baby with a dropper, but the squirrel would have none of it. That's when Embree had a brilliant idea. Her cat, Princess, had five babies of her own. Why not give her a sixth? Lisa's experiment was a "purrfect" success. Katherine Houpt, a Cornell University animal expert, said that it is not unusual for a cat to accept a foster child, but that Embree should not be surprised if the squirrel grows up believing it's a cat!

Mr. Mom: Six chicks were adopted by a rooster owned by Mary E. Harris of Tacoma, Washington. When the mother hen disappeared, the rooster rounded up the chicks, fed them, and then warmed and protected them.

Creature Feature

Yanto, a six-year-old who lives in Jakarta, Indonesia, frequently sleeps with the family pet, which is a . . .

a. panther.
b. monkey.
c. baby elephant.
d. python.

Body Heat: Cara Fligstein was buying pet food when she spied a cat and six nursing kittens nestled in a box in a corner of the pet store. A seventh kitten, much smaller than the rest, was too weak to nurse. Never

one to resist a kitten in need, Fligstein bought kitten formula and whisked the starving baby to the vet. The diagnosis? Severe dehydration. The kitten would have to be fed hourly and kept warm. Fligstein was assembling blankets and a heating pad when she realized that she wouldn't need them after all. Linus, her cairn terrier, was already keeping the kitten warm by allowing her to sleep on him. Three years later, Linus and Angel, the cat, are still the best of friends.

Mixed Company: Cattle and sheep usually don't mix, but when a group of lambs was penned in the same

pasture with cattle, the two species bonded so much that the cattle actually protected the sheep from predators.

The Fox and the Hound:

Foxhounds are trained to hunt foxes. But the foxhound and fox at the Belstone Hunt in England are an exception. Best buddies, the two animals follow each other around, eating and sleeping together and even drinking water from the same dish.

Blind Faith:

A victim of animal abuse, Little Ben, a Jack Russell terrier, is totally blind. People at the shelter in Essex, England, that rescued him were afraid he'd have to be put to sleep. But that was before Bill, another Jack Russell terrier, decided to befriend Ben. Bill allowed Ben to hang onto the back of his neck while he led him around the kennel to water and food dishes. When the local news stations broadcast the story, the shelter received more than 5,000 phone calls from people wanting to adopt the pair of dogs. It wasn't long before they were taken in by a woman with a big backyard and another little dog named Rosie to keep them company.

Horse Sense: Clever Hans, a horse, lived during the early 1900s. His owner, a math professor named Wilhelm von Osten, taught Hans how to spell and do simple mathematical problems. When von Osten tested his horse's knowledge, Clever Hans would nod his head for "yes," shake his head for "no," and stomp his feet to count out numbers. Visitors were amazed at how often Hans answered questions correctly. But then someone noticed that Hans only answered correctly if the questioner already knew the answer. It seems that Hans did not really know the answers, but was so sensitive to his human audience that he was able to pick up clues from a raised eyebrow, a sigh, or even a tilt of the head. Most people would consider that behavior quite clever as well!

Creature Feature

Dr. Hywell Williams of King's College Hospital in London has a patient who was alerted by her dog that she had . . .

a. severe bad breath.
b. athlete's foot.
c. tooth decay.
d. skin cancer.

Seizing the Moment: Because people with epilepsy often lose control of their bodies during a seizure, it's important for them to be somewhere safe. Epileptics have no idea when a seizure will strike, but research shows that dogs of various breeds, sizes, and ages are able to predict seizures. How they do it remains a mystery, but dogs like Brian Revheim's English setter, Arthur, can be trained to alert their owners minutes before an attack occurs.

Scents-sational! Dog-trainer Duane Pickel has trained a schnauzer named George to sniff out cancer before it can become a threat. After 8,000 hours of training, this talented canine correctly detected melanoma, the most dangerous form of skin cancer, 400 times out of 401 attempts.

Creature Feature

Penny, a Doberman pinscher, alerts her owner that she is about to have a seizure by . . .

a. pushing her into a chair.
b. bringing her a pillow.
c. banging on the piano.
d. hiding her car keys.

Sixth Scents: In his book, *Dogs That Know When Their Owners Are Coming Home*, Rupert Sheldrake writes about telepathic behavior between animals and their owners. One of his subjects, an English hospital worker named Gloria Batabyal, was

puzzled by the fact that her husband always had a piping hot cup of tea waiting for her when she arrived home, even though her schedule was unpredictable. How did he know when to put the kettle on? The couple's two dogs always ran to the window at the exact moment she left the hospital, giving her husband just enough time to prepare the tea.

Phoning Home: When Veronica Rowe's daughter Marian left for college, she had no choice but to leave

her adoring cat, Carlo, home with her family. Mysteriously, whenever she called, Carlo would perk up and rush over to the phone before anyone had even answered. No one else ever knew when Marian was phoning, but Carlo's instincts were right every time!

Sweet Homecoming:

Sugar, a cream-colored Persian cat, is the star of a study published by J. B. Rhine of Duke University. Of all the cases he documented in which animals find their owners over long distances, Rhine was most impressed by Sugar, who jumped out of the family car and disappeared before they moved from California to Oklahoma. One day, Sugar just showed up at her owners' new home, having traveled 1,000 miles to find them!

Visiting Hours: During the 1960s, a 12-year boy from West Virginia found a racing pigeon in his backyard. It was wearing a leg ring with the number 167. After the boy fed it, the pigeon stuck around and soon became the boy's pet. No one knew how devoted the bird had become until the boy was hospitalized 105 miles from home. Recovering from an operation in his room, the boy heard a familiar noise at the window. He asked the nurse to open the window, and in flew a pigeon. On its leg was a ring with the number 167!

Prince of Tides: During World War I, when Private James Brown of England was sent overseas to France, his dog, Prince, was heartbroken. Imagine Brown's surprise when Prince came trotting up to him in the trenches! No one could figure out how the dog got there. The only possible explanation was that Prince had boarded a ship full of soldiers wearing the same uniform as his master. Brown's commanding officer was so impressed by the dog's loyalty that he allowed Prince to stay by his master's side for the rest of the war!

Creature Feature

At the Anderson House Hotel in Wabash, Minnesota, visitors can . . .

a. bring their pets into the restaurant.
b. request pet-sitting service.
c. milk the cows for fresh milk in the morning.
d. reserve a cat to keep them company for the night.

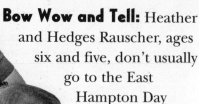

Bow Wow and Tell: Heather and Hedges Rauscher, ages six and five, don't usually go to the East Hampton Day Care Center. But they were there on the day their mother had a meeting, and volunteers from the Animal Rescue Fund brought dogs in to show the children. When the dogs arrived, Heather cried, "That's Cody!" It turned out that Cody had disappeared from the girls' home three months earlier. The folks at the animal shelter said that Cody hadn't acted like a stray, wagging his tail or licking visitors. Maybe he was just waiting for a day like this one!

Horseback Therapy: Patients at the Akron Children's Hospital in Ohio look forward to the days when a miniature horse named Petie comes to visit. Petie gives them rides or pulls them down the hall in their wheelchairs, his handlers walking alongside.

Creature Feature

It has been demonstrated that stroking a pet can . . .

a. lower blood pressure.
b. cure mental illness.
c. induce weight loss.
d. increase one's IQ.

Fin-tastic! Dolphins have enchanted people for thousands of years. Now there is evidence that young people who suffer from autism and have serious trouble bonding with others show marked improvement when in the company of these playful creatures. Dolphins seem to be able to sense just what autistic children need and are less rambunctious with them than they are with their trainers. After just a few sessions, Rafi, an 18-year-old autistic patient at the Aytanim home for the handicapped in Israel, spoke a few words for the first time in his life.

Puppy Love: Gayle Bardin-Aversa, an occupational therapist with Therapy Dogs International, says that she can get better results from patients when she uses a six-year-old Yorkshire terrier named Zoey. For example, one four-year-old boy found it painful to use his disabled left hand and no one could get him to try. But when Bardin-Aversa placed Zoey in the boy's lap and asked him to brush her, he eagerly grasped the brush with his left hand. Clearly, Zoey had provided more motivation than anyone else could.

Horsing Around:

Taking pet devotion to new heights, The Maltese Cat, a thoroughbred race horse, was chosen by his trainer, Terry Lee Griffith of Stanton, Delaware, to be the best man at his wedding. The horse wore formal attire, including a top hat!

Creature Feature

Bred in Australia, a new type of dog combining the friendliness of one breed with the intelligence of a poodle is called a . . .

a. schnoodle (schnauzer and poodle).
b. labradoodle (Labrador retriever and poodle).
c. cockapoo (cocker spaniel and poodle).
d. pugadoodle (pug and poodle).

Chimp Change:

When an elderly Danish woman died, she left her entire life savings to six creatures who were dear to her heart. Jimmy, Trunto, Trine, Fifi, Grimmi, and Gigi, chimpanzees at the Copenhagen Zoo, were suddenly $60,000 richer! Now that's a lot of bananas!

Big Woof: Now there's a must-have device for dog lovers who are experiencing a communication gap. The Bowlingual, available in Japan, claims to translate those meaningful woofs uttered by your pooch into human words! Tone, pitch, volume, and other barking patterns are matched to canine emotions, which then appear as words on the Bowlingual computer screen.

Pampered Pet Set: The ad in the telephone book boasts air-conditioned private rooms for pampered pets as well as a fully furnished two-bedroom apartment. The Malibu Pet Hotel has something for everyone—everyone with four legs, that is. Furry guests enjoy daily five-mile walks, grooming, and lots of chew toys. Their wagging tails are certain to reassure two-legged owners that their pets are more than well cared for.

Pet Detective:

When Carol Piccione lost Shadow, her two-year-old black Labrador retriever mix, she was inconsolable. She went to the local animal shelter twice a day and circled the neighborhood in her car for days on end. She had

almost given up when, a month later, she was driving by another animal shelter farther from her home and something told her to go in. There was Shadow—Piccione had found him just 15 minutes before he was scheduled to be put to sleep! Not wanting others to go through what she did, Piccione started Animal Lost & Found, Inc. For a fee, Piccione will devote her considerable skills to locating a lost pet. Though she refuses to divulge her secrets, she pretty much has the process down to a science. Just ask the owners of Stella, Bowser, Cupcake, and Mischka!

Creature Feature

Pet detective Lori Ketcham's most unusual case involved locating a lost . . .

a. giraffe.
b. potbelly pig.
c. emu.
d. ferret.

They say that opposites attract—and it seems especially true in the animal kingdom. But one of the following animal pairs stands alone—as being totally false!

a. Who would have thought that porcupines and coyotes could be the best of friends? Coyotes share their food with porcupines and, in exchange, their prickly buddies will happily scratch their backs.

Believe It!   **Not!**

b. Honeyguide birds need the help of honey badgers to retrieve sweet nectar from beehives. The bird will flutter around the badger until it digs out the honey from the hive, leaving the honeycomb for its feathered friend.

Believe It!   **Not!**

c. In 2002, people in Kenya were shocked to see a lioness mothering two baby oryxes, an animal she would normally eat for lunch.

Believe It!   **Not!**

d. In the shallow water of tide pools lives a strange pair—the blind shrimp and the goby. The shrimp digs the burrow that the two will share, while the goby keeps an eye out—because the shrimp can't see at all.

Believe It!   **Not!**

BONUS QUESTION—WILDLIFE WONDER

A penguin was brought from Greenland to the National Zoo in Washington, D.C. Lonesome for home, the penguin befriended a polar bear in the next cage over and refused to leave its side.

Believe It!   **Not!**

Many animal species are in danger of becoming extinct. It's a good thing that there are people devoted to keeping them alive.

Breeding Grounds: In recent years, the purpose of zoos has shifted from family entertainment to preserving species in danger of extinction—and with good reason. The tropical rain forest that contains the greatest percentage of the world's animal species is disappearing at a rate of 50 acres per minute!

Creature Feature

There are more of these animals in zoos today than in all of Asia.

a. Pandas
b. Siberian tigers
c. Rhesus monkeys
d. Red-crowned cranes

Frozen Zoo: The San Diego Zoo keeps some of their animals in freezers—not whole animals, of course, but their cells. Four storage tanks hold the cells of more than 4,000 animals. The cells are frozen in liquid

nitrogen to prevent the formation of ice crystals, which would tear the cells during thawing. Thawed without ice crystals, cells remain unharmed and can even grow again.

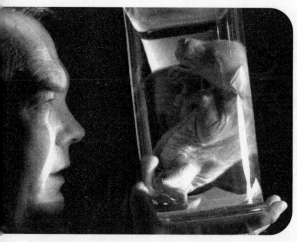

Coming Back to Life: In 1936, the Tasmanian tiger became extinct. Every last one had been hunted down by farmers who blamed the wolf-sized marsupial for killing their sheep. Recently, Mike Archer, director of the Australian Museum in Sydney, took steps to clone the animal. In May 2000, a research team extracted DNA from a pup that had been preserved in formaldehyde for the museum's collection. It may not be long until the call of the Tasmanian tiger is heard again.

Are You My Mommy? In 1986, there were only three California condors living in the wild and 12 others living at the Los Angeles Zoo. Hoping to increase their numbers, zoologists decided to try breeding them in captivity. In the wild, condors lay a single egg every other year. But at the zoo, their caregivers whisk the eggs away and put them into incubators, hoping that the condors will lay more. Because baby birds think that whoever feeds them is their parent, caregivers wear condor hand puppets so that the babies won't get attached to them. Today, there are 36 condors living in the wild and 115 in captivity.

Creature Feature

Without zoos and their breeding centers, this animal would be as dead as a dinosaur.

a. European bison
b. Bald eagle
c. Mountain gorilla
d. Hippopotamus

Bearing Up: A polar bear named Gus is the main attraction at the Central Park Zoo in New York City. But fame was not enough to make him happy. Obsessively swimming from one end of his pool to the other, Gus was clearly suffering from boredom. The zookeepers decided to cheer him up with a brand-new $25,000 Jacuzzi. Fighting the strong current and rushing water seemed to perk Gus up. But it was the "bearcicles," fish coated with peanut butter and frozen inside a block of ice, that really did wonders for his mood!

Scaredy Cat: In an effort to entertain Nikki, a Siberian tiger at the Oregon Zoo, caretakers put a trout in her pool. But although many tigers like to fish, Nikki ignored the fish—until it leaped out of the water. Startled, the big cat jumped right out of the pool! The ball her keepers gave her next was much more to her liking.

Creature Feature

Counting just mammals and birds, our planet loses one species every . . .

a. five years.
b. ten years.
c. 18 months.
d. eight months.

Well-Oiled Operation:

When a tanker spill polluted South African waters with oil in June 2000, the lives of more than 40,000 penguins were threatened. The oil that covered the penguins from head to toe stripped the feathers of their natural waterproofing, and left the penguins waterlogged and in danger of freezing. Thousands of volunteers worked as fast as they could to move the birds to the mainland, where they could be warmed up and fed. When the penguins were strong enough, volunteers scrubbed their feathers with soap and toothbrushes. As soon as water began to bead up on their feathers, the penguins were released. The biggest bird rescue ever attempted was a roaring success!

Hog Heaven: Diablo, a warthog at the San Antonio Zoo in Texas, got his name (which means "devil" in Spanish) from his habit of growling and charging at his caregivers. But everything changed when turnips and sweet potatoes were buried in his outdoor pen. Diablo kicked up his heels with joy as he gathered the hidden treats. Apparently he wasn't mean at all—just bored or hungry for his favorite foods.

Tons of Love: Husband-and-wife team Scott Riddle and Heidi Strommer Riddle, former zookeepers from Los Angeles, have achieved their dream—Riddle's Elephant Breeding Farm and Wildlife Sanctuary in Arkansas. This nonprofit sanctuary takes in any elephant that needs a home, from retired circus performers to cantankerous zoo misfits. And then there's Solomon, an orphaned, unruly calf from Zimbabwe. Under the Riddles' care, he has morphed into a gentle giant who entertains visitors by playing the harmonica!

Creature Feature

In 1976, there were only about 5,000 harbor seals left in the wild. With the passage of the Marine Mammal Protection Act of 1972, which made it a crime to kill the seals, their numbers have increased to about . . .

a. 10,000.
b. 15,000.
c. 25,000.
d. 30,000.

Marine Biology: The Kemp's Ridley turtle is the smallest and rarest of sea turtles. In fact, it's so scarce that the Mexican government sent Marines to guard the only beach on which it nests.

Lofty Goal: When large fish hawks called ospreys wound up on the New York State endangered species list, some bird lovers went into the nest-building business. Ospreys had begun to disappear for two reasons. First, the use of the insecticide DDT weakened their eggs, causing them to crack open before the chicks were ready to hatch. And second, because of a shortage of suitable nesting areas, the birds began to build nests on utility poles, prompting utility workers to get rid of the nests. Now, thanks to a ban on DDT and the efforts of volunteers who construct nesting platforms, ospreys are making a comeback.

Snug as a Bug: Orphaned kangaroos and wallabies are quite common in Australia because the mothers don't always make it across the highways. Tailor-made by a conservation group, soft, warm "Joey bags" help the orphaned babies feel safe until they are old enough to face the world on their own.

Egg-o-centric: Because white-naped cranes are seriously endangered, bird experts tried to hatch eggs from captive cranes in incubators. When the project failed, Fred Koontz of the New York Zoological Society came up with a biotelemetric egg—a plastic Easter egg fitted with a battery-operated transmitter—to study nesting practices in the wild. An "eggs-traordinary" success, the egg recorded such things as temperature, humidity, and the number of times it was turned over by the mother bird. The result? Vital information that may increase the ability to hatch eggs laid in captivity.

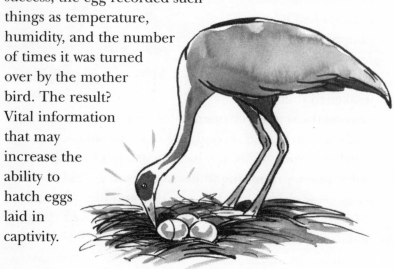

Good News: Scientists thought that the black-footed ferret, once common on the prairie, was extinct. Then in 1981, a small group was discovered on a Wyoming ranch. After a captive breeding program at the Wyoming Zoo, about 200 ferrets were reintroduced to their natural habitat. Several litters have been born in the wild, and scientists are hopeful that this species will soon be off the endangered list.

Toad-ally Alarming:

Scientists concerned about Earth's environment are taking their cues from frogs and toads. Because they drink and breathe through their skin, these animals are very vulnerable to pesticides, fertilizers, and other pollutants that can eventually hurt people as well. Recently, frogs and toads around the world have begun to disappear. Many others are born with deformities. Luckily, scientists are on the case. They know that solving the mystery of the disappearing frogs and toads will solve some problems for people as well.

Chips Ahoy! Microcomputer technology has become so advanced that tiny birds and toads can be fitted with mini transmitters so biologists can track them by satellite instead of on foot. Scientists think it won't be long now before the equipment will be light enough to attach to a bee!

Creature Feature

For the first time ever recorded, a pair of red-tailed hawks has been observed nesting on . . .

a. a tall building on New York City's Fifth Avenue.
b. the Golden Gate Bridge in California.
c. the Eiffel Tower in Paris.
d. St. Peter's Basilica in Rome.

Fish-eye Lens: Marine biologist Greg Marshall was deep-sea diving when he saw a shark swim by with a smaller fish attached to it by its suction-cuplike lips. Marshall, a photographer for the National Geographic Society, had a flash of inspiration. "What if I substituted a video camera for the shark-sucker?" So Marshall invented the Crittercam. First designed to get a shark's-eye view of the sea, the Crittercam has since been attached to a variety of other sea creatures, many of them endangered. The Hawaiian monk seal has already benefited. Crittercam videos showed scientists that these animals hunt for food a lot deeper and farther away in the ocean than they had thought. Now the monk seals' waters are protected and their future looks a lot rosier.

Creature Feature

In 2001, an ultralight airplane led a flock of rare young birds from Wisconsin to Florida, where they spent the winter, then successfully flew back on their own. What is this endangered species?

a. Brown pelicans
b. Blue-footed boobies
c. Passenger pigeons
d. Whooping cranes

Brain Buster

Scientists have proven that animals in the wild know certain remedies to keep themselves healthy. Which one of these animal survival stories is a sham?

a. Generations of elephants in Kenya have mined special caves near a volcano to get at soft rock that is particularly high in vitamins and minerals.
Believe It!   **Not!**

b. Mosquitoes will not suck the blood of people with colds or illnesses.
Believe It!   **Not!**

c. Chimpanzees with gastrointestinal problems have been known to bite clay off of termite mounds to treat their illness.
Believe It!   **Not!**

d. Capuchin monkeys in Costa Rica have been known to rub a type of chili plant on their fur to ward off insects.
Believe It!   **Not!**

BONUS QUESTION—WILDLIFE WONDER

Skunk spray is actually antibacterial in nature. The skunk not only uses it as a defense mechanism, but also sprays its young to keep them free from germs.

Believe It!   **Not!**

CHAPTER 5 To the Rescue!

The courage of animals in the face of danger should never be underestimated.

Tree Service: In 1942, Captain Cyril Jones parachuted into the Sumatran jungle. Entangled in the branches of a tree, he was unable to free himself for 12 days. Jones survived with the help of a monkey, who brought him fruit to eat. When Jones did get free, he was soon captured and taken to a prison camp. The little monkey followed, attacking anyone who bullied him. Afraid that his captors would shoot the monkey, Jones shooed it away, probably saving its life.

Creature Feature

The American Rescue Dog Association, located in Seattle, Washington, prefers using this breed of dog in search and rescue operations:

a. collie.
b. Newfoundland.
c. Saint Bernard.
d. German shepherd.

Pulling More Than Her Own Weight: One cold winter day, 36-year-old Michael Miller took Sadie, his English setter, out hunting. Suddenly, a third of a mile into the woods, Miller had a heart attack. He called Sadie with a whistle, then fell to the ground. Unable to walk, Miller held onto Sadie's collar—and the 45-pound dog dragged her 180-pound owner, now semiconscious, all the way back home.

Miller's wife called for an ambulance, and he was rushed to the hospital for emergency surgery. Without Sadie's help, Miller might never have made it out of the woods.

Pig Tale: The day two burglars forced their way into Rebecca Moyer's home, her 300-pound pet pig was taking a snooze in the kitchen. When Arnold heard his owner's screams, he came to the rescue, chomping on one of the bad guy's legs—and sending both crooks scurrying away in fear.

Creature Feature

Rescue dogs work hard to find people buried in debris caused by earthquakes and other disasters, but if they can't find anyone who's alive, they get depressed. To make them feel better, their handlers might . . .

a. bury another worker and let the dog think it's found a live victim.

b. take it for a walk near a peaceful lake.

c. give it a break and let it play with the other rescue dogs.

d. take it out for a big steak dinner.

Porpoise with a Purpose: From 1790 to 1810, a white porpoise named Hatteras Jack guided every ship in and out of Hatteras Inlet, off the coast of North Carolina, and never lost a single vessel.

Shell Shock:

Candelaria Villanueva was thrown into the sea when the ship she was on sank 600 miles south of Manila. Until she was rescued two days later, she was kept afloat by a giant sea turtle. A smaller turtle bit her whenever her head began to droop into the water.

Kitty Pity: Ginny, a dog owned by Philip Gonzalez, seeks out and rescues stray cats from dumpsters, air-conditioning ducts, and other dangerous places. Sometimes she rescues as many as eight injured cats in a week, and hundreds of cats owe their lives to her. There's even a charity named after this heroic dog, the Ginny Fund, that provides money to help cats find good homes and pay their veterinary bills.

Gorilla Posse: When a poacher kidnapped an infant gorilla from its mother, 60 gorillas banded together to get the baby back. In the middle of the night, they invaded a  little village on the border of what was once Equatorial Africa. Ignoring the gunshots fired by villagers, the gorillas banged angrily on doors and windows. Finally, the village chief learned who the poacher was and ordered him to return the kidnapped baby. Appeased, the posse turned around and headed for the forest, beating their chests and screeching with joy.

Breath Saver: Judi Bayly of Nashua, New Hampshire, has a breathing disorder that requires her to wear an oxygen mask while she's sleeping. One night in 1996, Bayly's mask slipped from her face. Lyric, her Irish setter, sprang into action just as he'd been taught. Unable to rouse Bayly, he ran to the phone, knocked the receiver off the hook, and hit the button for 911 three times. When an EMS worker answered, Lyric barked into the receiver and help was soon on its way. The workers who revived Bayly said that they had arrived just in the nick of time.

Creature Feature

In a museum in Italy, there is a statue dating back to the Roman Empire that depicts . . .

a. a lion rescuing a little girl lost in the forest.
b. two large dogs saving drowning people from the sea.
c. three children riding an elephant.
d. a dog dragging a baby from a burning building.

Tag Team: One cold winter day, Chris Georgiou decided to catch up on some yard work at his trout-fishing farm in Australia. Ziggy, his border collie, kept him company, while Stella, his rottweiler, napped about 60 yards away. When Georgiou stood up to rest his back, he banged his head on the railing around the fishing area, lost his balance, and slipped into the icy water. Georgiou couldn't swim, and his heavy clothes weighed him down. Perhaps Ziggy knew that she was too light to pull him out because she stayed nearby, barking frantically to waken Stella. Within seconds, Stella hurtled into the lake, where Georgiou was able to grab her leg and hold on as she towed him to shallow water.

Attack Cat:

Michael Talbot was awakened from a sound sleep by a crash in the next room. He got up to investigate and found an intruder riffling through his possessions. The armed thief ordered Talbot to go back to bed. Not about to argue, Talbot was leaving when Nicky, his gentle, affectionate cat, bolted into the room, growling and hissing. She hurled herself at the intruder, scratching and biting his face. The thief ran, eager to get away from Nicky as fast as possible.

Creature Feature

A statue of a dog named Balto stands in New York City's Central Park to commemorate Balto's work . . .

a. with the New York City Fire Department.

b. delivering medicine to the sick during one of Alaska's worst blizzards.

c. saving hundreds of lives in the Johnstown flood.

d. locating victims in the debris after the Oklahoma City bombing.

Smoke Detector: When actor Drew Barrymore's house caught on fire in February 2001, she was sound asleep in her bedroom. It's a good thing Flossie, Barrymore's Labrador retriever–chow mix, awakened her in time for her to get out before the fire raged through the house.

No Joke: In his early teens, when psychic Uri Geller was living in Cyprus, one of his favorite pastimes was to explore the caves in the hills above his school. One day, Geller went exploring by himself and got lost deep within the caves. He was cold and wet and nothing looked familiar. Worse still, the batteries in his flashlight were about to run out. Geller knew that two of his classmates had gotten lost in the caves and starved to death. Terrified, he had all but given up hope when he felt two paws on his chest. It was his dog, Joker! Geller had no idea how his dog knew where to find him or that he needed finding. But Joker knew the way out, and that's all that mattered.

School of Hard Knocks: When a school of dolphins began to go berserk in the waters just south of Brisbane, Australia, three surfers didn't know what to make of it. Why were the dolphins suddenly diving under their surfboards and poking at them with their noses? Then 17-year-old Adam Maguire saw a shark charging toward him! He punched it in the head and jumped on his board. But the shark came after him, taking a bite out of his board and his hip and knocking Adam into the water as his friends watched in horror. Suddenly, the dolphins went into a frenzy, beating the water with their tails. The distraction gave Adam just enough time to crawl back on his board and float back to shore on the next wave. Adam was airlifted to a hospital, where doctors performed life-saving surgery.

Creature Feature

Scientists have determined that the genetic makeup of humans is most similar to that of . . .

a. pigs.
b. horses.
c. dolphins.
d. chimpanzees.

Pig Power: Priscilla was as happy as a pig could be, swimming with her owner in a lake near Houston, Texas. Suddenly, she was distracted by the panicked cries of 11-year-old Anthony Melton, who was starting to drown. Priscilla took off in his direction and, when she was close enough, began to nudge him with her snout. The sight of a pig in the water jolted Anthony out of his panic long enough for him to grab Priscilla's harness so she could tow him to shore. In 1995, in honor of her super-porcine efforts as a lifeguard, Priscilla became the first animal to be inducted into the Texas Veterinary Medical Association's Hall of Fame.

Creature Feature

Dolphins protect their babies from predators by . . .

a. beating attackers with their snouts.
b. scaring enemies with high-pitched screeches.
c. beating the water with their tails.
d. hiding their babies in seaweed.

Heroes come in all different shapes and sizes—some even have tails and fur! Three of these remarkable animal rescue stories are true. Can you find the phony?

a. Binti Jua, a gorilla in the Brookfield Zoo in Chicago, Illinois, rescued a three-year-old boy who fell 18 feet into her enclosure.

Believe It!   Not!

b. In 1890, a rabbit named Misty followed thieves who had burglarized its owner's house. When the owner returned with the police, Misty led them to the thieves' hideout.

Believe It!   Not!

c. In 1980, a dog named Woody jumped off an 80-foot cliff into a river to save a woman from drowning. Woody kept her afloat until help arrived.

Believe It!   Not!

d. Scarlett, a stray cat in Brooklyn, New York, hurried in and out of a burning building over and over again, until she had rescued all five of her kittens.

Believe It!   Not!

BONUS QUESTION—WILDLIFE WONDER

A dentist in Illinois once saved the life of a fish. The golden puffer's teeth had grown so big that the fish could not eat. The dentist filed down its teeth so that the fish could eat again.

Believe It!   **Not!**

POP QUIZ

Think you know everything about these awesome animals? Well, test your smarts with this final Brain Buster. It's a review of the wild and crazy animal facts collected in this book. Ready to go, Tiger?

1. Which of these hard-to-believe food-gathering stories is truly false?
a. Chimpanzees use tools to poke into termite mounds and scare them out.
b. Sea otters bang abalone shells against a rock balanced on their stomach until the shells break open.
c. Vultures crack open the tough shells of ostrich eggs by dropping rocks on them.
d. It takes a penguin seven years to learn to fish with a seaweed net.

2. One of the following animal stories speaks the truth. The rest are false. Can you spot the unbelievable reality?
a. Matt and Cyndi Goodie own a rather musical Yorkshire terrier named Coquito that barks, in key, along with more than 200 different songs.
b. Professor Irene Pepperberg's African gray parrot knows 100 words and can identify 50 different objects.
c. Brooklyn zoologist Craig Morris has trained a team of seals to understand vocal commands. Strangely, the seals only respond to the words when they are sung.
d. Ten-year-old Julie Shermak taught her pet mongoose, Sweetie, to say, "Rock on!"

3. Elephants communicate across long distances by . . .

a. stomping on the ground.

b. sending certain birds to act as messengers.

c. bellowing into trees.

d. sending plant leaves down rivers.

4. Male black-capped chickadees have singing contests to decide who gets to mate with the most females.

Believe It! **Not!**

5. Juan Solis of Bolivia, who was blind, was guided by a . . .

a. tortoise.

b. goat.

c. coyote.

d. cat.

6. During World War II, the United States used what kind of bird to deliver secret messages?

a. Sparrow

b. Eagle

c. Turkey

d. Pigeon

7. A fox and a hound *can* be friends! And at the Belstone Hunt in England, such an unlikely pair exists.

Believe It! **Not!**

8. Bill, a Jack Russell terrier, helps Ben, another Jack Russell terrier, get around because Ben can't . . .

a. bark.

b. see.

c. hear.

d. smell.

9. Which of these amazing lost-and-found stories is true?

a. Three siblings from California were surfing in Hawaii when a current took their boards far out to sea. A school of dolphins escorted the unharmed teens to shore— right back to the hotel where they were staying.

b. English Private James Brown's dog, Prince, found his master in France during World War II. Apparently, the dog boarded a ship carrying soldiers wearing uniforms like Private Brown's.

c. Stephanie Silvs, an actress from Buffalo, New York, set out on a cross-country tour after leaving her dog, Daisy, with friends. But when the tour ended in Orlando, Florida, there was Daisy, waiting at Silvs's hotel!

d. Italian veterinarian Alexis Fermanis was hiking on a mountain trail when she fell off a cliff. She was knocked unconscious and woke up with amnesia. Luckily, when one of her patients, a clever Labrador retriever, found Fermanis in the hospital, she regained her memory completely.

10. What kind of animal was best man at Terry Lee Griffith's wedding in Stanton, Delaware?

a. A dog
b. A monkey
c. A horse
d. A parrot

11. The tropical rain forests that contain the greatest percentage of the world's animal species are disappearing at a rate of . . .

a. 10 acres per minute.
b. 20 acres per minute.
c. 40 acres per minute.
d. 50 acres per minute.

12. Which zany zoo story is totally untrue?

a. Diablo, an unhappy warthog in Texas, was cheered up when turnips and sweet potatoes were buried in his pen.

b. A polar bear named Gus found a cure for boredom when his zoo pool was turned into a Jacuzzi.

c. Nikki, a Siberian tiger, was scared when the trout in her pool started jumping.

d. A monkey named Max loved the scooters that kids rode outside his cage. When scooters were banned, Max got so depressed, his handlers bought him one of his own!

13. Frogs are very vulnerable to pollution because . . .

a. they drink and breathe through their skin.

b. the flies they eat are carriers.

c. they are attracted to polluted swamps.

d. their eyes are always open.

14. Candelaria Villanueva was thrown into the sea, but kept afloat for two days by a pig.

Believe It!　　　　Not!

15. Which one of these four animal alarm stories is not alarming at all (because it's not true!)?

a. Rebecca Moyer's pet pig chomped on the leg of a burglar, sending the two thieves running away.

b. When Anat Leonard fell asleep with a candle burning by her bedside, her goldfish jumped out of its bowl and flung itself onto Leonard's pillow. Leonard woke up, put the fish back in its bowl, and blew out the candle.

c. Michael Talbot's cat, Nicky, hurled herself at a late-night burglar, causing him to run away.

d. Drew Barrymore's pet dog woke her up when her house caught fire.

Answer Key

Chapter 1
Smarter Than You Think!
Page 5:   **c.** frightened.

Page 6:   **a.** sponges.

Page 9:   **c.** is infected with *Toxoplasma gondii*.

Page 11:   **a.** when they are shown photos.

Page 12:   **b.** watching the flight patterns of other birds.

Page 15:   **a.** squawked "boat."

Page 17:   **d.** understand fractions.

Page 18:   **d.** build castles with Lego toys.

Page 20:   **a.** an orangutan that regularly dismantles
his cage.

Brain Buster: d. is false.

Bonus Question: Believe It!

Chapter 2
Can-do Critters
Page 23:   **a.** 300-pound ostrich.

Page 25:   **a.** an ordained minister.

Page 27:   **c.** camels pulling a car with no engine.

Page 29:   **a.** Bear Field, because a trained bear was
used to clear the construction site.

Page 30:   **b.** trim the White House lawn.

Page 32:   **d.** pigs in pantaloons dancing to bagpipes.

Brain Buster: c. is false.

Bonus Question: Believe It!

Chapter 3
Helping Hands & Friendly Paws

Page 35: **b.** 25 chicks.

Page 36: **d.** python.

Page 39: **d.** skin cancer.

Page 40: **a.** pushing her into a chair.

Page 43: **d.** reserve a cat to keep them company for the night.

Page 44: **a.** lower blood pressure.

Page 46: **b.** labradoodle (Labrador retriever and poodle).

Page 48: **c.** emu.

Brain Buster: a. is false.

Bonus Question: Not!

Chapter 4
Good Breeding

Page 51: **b.** Siberian tigers

Page 53: **a.** European bison

Page 54: **d.** eight months.

Page 56: **d.** 30,000.

Page 59: **a.** a tall building on New York City's Fifth Avenue.

Page 60: **d.** Whooping cranes

Brain Buster: b. is false.

Bonus Question: Not!

Chapter 5
To the Rescue

Page 63:   **d.** German shepherd.

Page 64:   **a.** bury another worker and let the dog think it's found a live victim.

Page 67:   **b.** two large dogs saving drowning people from the sea.

Page 69:   **b.** delivering medicine to the sick during one of Alaska's worst blizzards.

Page 71:   **c.** dolphins.

Page 72:   **c.** beating the water with their tails.

Brain Buster: **b.** is false.

Bonus Question: Believe It!

Pop Quiz

1.   **d.**
2.   **b.**
3.   **a.**
4.   **Believe It!**
5.   **a.**
6.   **d.**
7.   **Believe It!**
8.   **b.**
9.   **b.**
10.   **c.**
11.   **d.**
12.   **d.**
13.   **a.**
14.   **Not!**
15.   **b.**

What's Your Ripley's Rank?

Ripley's Scorecard

Congratulations! You've done a whale of a job spotting fictions among all these amazing animal facts! Now it's time to tally up your answers and get your Ripley's rating. Are you **Catnapping on the Job**? Or are you **Like a Fish in the Sea**? Add up your scores to find out.

Here's the scoring breakdown. Give yourself:

★ **10 points** for every **Creature Feature** you got right;

★ **20 points** for every fiction you spotted in the **Ripley's Brain Busters**;

★ **10 points** every time you solved a **Wildlife Wonder**;

★ and **5 points** for every **Pop Quiz** question you answered correctly.

Here's a tally sheet:

Number of **Creature Feature**
questions answered correctly: _____ x 10 = _____

Number of **Ripley's Brain Buster**
fictions spotted: _____ x 20 = _____

Number of **Wildlife Wonder**
questions solved: _____ x 10 = _____

Number of **Pop Quiz** questions
answered correctly: _____ x 5 = _____

Total the right column for your final score: _____

0–100
Catnapping on the Job?

Rise and shine and welcome to the world of Robert Ripley! There are amazing, unbelievable facts all around you, and it's time you started taking notice. The animal kingdom is just one place to find extraordinary happenings. Inventors, bugs, history—there are weird and wacky elements to just about every subject in the world—but only if you decide to look!

101–250
Doggone Amazing!

You are pawing your way along, learning all about the amazing animal kingdom. Now we just have to better acquaint you with Robert Ripley's collection of all things bizarre and unusual. That way you'll be able to tell the unbelievable from the untrue—a very difficult distinction in Ripley's world!

251–400
No Monkey Business

You are getting serious about the wild and wacky animal kingdom. No slipping any funky fictions by you—you've got a great grasp of the unbelievable! How did you learn so much about the unusual? You must be a Ripley's regular. Which means you know that there are all kinds of bizarre stories out there!

401–575
Like a Fish in the Sea

They say that elephants never forget, and neither do you! You have an amazing knack for wacky animal facts. And you can easily tell when someone is just monkeying around with fake answers! You are at the top of the Ripley's food chain—and for good reason!

Believe It!®

Photo Credits

Ripley Entertainment Inc. and the editors of this book wish to thank the following photographers, agents, and other individuals for permission to use and reprint the following photographs in this book. Any photographs included in this book that are not acknowledged below are property of the Ripley Archives. Great effort has been made to obtain permission from the owners of all materials included in this book. Any errors that may have been made are unintentional and will gladly be corrected in future printings if notice is sent to Ripley Entertainment Inc., 5728 Major Boulevard, Orlando, Florida 32819.

7 Sea Otter; 15 Elephant; 18 Black-capped Chickadee; 53 Baby Condor and Hand Puppet; 59 Frog/U.S. Fish and Wildlife Service

12 Azy/Jessie Cohen/National Zoological Park/Smithsonian Institution

17 Lions Attacking Wildebeest/Al Robinson

24 Ping/Courtesy Michele Brown

26 Seeing Eye Dog/KRT

28 Dan Shaw and Cuddles/Courtesy Janet Burleson

30 Capuchin Monkey/PhotoDisc

37 Linus and Angel/Mary Packard

39 Clever Hans/Copyright Unknown/From the Book *Clever Hans* by Oskar Pfungst/New York, Henry Holt and Company, 1911

40 Brian Revheim and Arthur/Megan Revheim

42 Racing Pigeon/Courtesy Paul Walsh/http://walshloft.com

44 The Rauschers and Cody; 48 Carol Piccione and Shadow/© 2002 Newsday, Inc./Reprinted with Permission

45 Dolphins/Hemera

47 Dog Wearing Bowlingual/Takara Co., Ltd.

52 Mike Archer and Tasmanian Tiger; 55 Penguin Rescue/Reuters Photo Archive

64 Michael Miller and Sadie/PR Newswire Photo Service

70 Drew Barrymore/Zuma Press

Contents

Introduction

The Ripley Experience

Robert Ripley started his career as a sports cartoonist for the *New York Globe* newspaper. One day he was having a hard time thinking of a cartoon to draw and his deadline was fast approaching. Suddenly a great idea popped into his head. Ripley dug into his files of unusual sports achievements, then quickly sketched nine of the more interesting and unusual items— and the first Believe It or Not! cartoon was born.

The cartoon was such a hit that Ripley's editor asked him to do more. Hoping that people would enjoy reading about other bizarre topics, Ripley expanded his column. Soon he was searching the globe for the weirdest things he could find. And what could be more bizarre than bugs?

Since bug behavior is among the strangest on Earth, Ripley had a steady supply of bug facts to showcase in his cartoons. Take the bombardier beetle, which sets off foul-smelling stink bombs from its backside, sending its enemies running for cover. Or the potter ant, which spends hours and hours fashioning small mud pots, one for each of her eggs. And there's the wasp that paralyzes a tarantula and buries it with one of her eggs so her soon-to-be hatched baby will have plenty of fresh food to eat. The list is endless.

Even the most common bugs are extraordinary. Everyone knows that caterpillars turn into butterflies or moths. But did you know that the young, or *nymph*, of the dragonfly lives underwater and is so fierce it can capture and eat small fish? Or that a tiny flea can jump as high as a foot—about 150 times its own body length?

Ripley was also fascinated by success stories, and bugs

are the most successful creatures on Earth. More than a million species of insects have been identified, and new ones are being discovered all the time. Making up more than five sixths of all living creatures, bugs are found everywhere, from deserts to rain forests, from hot springs to glaciers. And consider this: humans have never once been able to wipe out a single species of bug. Think of the cockroach. It was here before the dinosaurs—and it's still around today!

When asked where he got his facts, Ripley always replied, "Everywhere, and all the time. It's impossible to run dry on astonishing facts about our world." How many astonishing facts do you know about bugs? Find out by taking the Jeepers Creepers! quizzes and the Ripley's Brain Buster in each chapter. Then try the Pop Quiz at the end of the book and use the scorecard to figure out your Ripley's rank.

Welcome to the truly amazing world of bugs. It will be your strangest adventure yet.

Believe It!®

What's so bizarre about bugs? A better question might be: "What *isn't?*"

Body Count: The best way to figure out if a bug is an insect is to count its body sections. Insects' bodies are divided into three main parts: head, thorax, and abdomen. Centipedes and millipedes have lots of body sections, and spiders have just two. You can also count legs. Insects have six legs, spiders have eight, centipedes can have nearly 200 legs, and worms have no legs at all.

Jeepers Creepers!

Scientists say that for every human on Earth there are . . .

a. one million insects.
b. 200 million insects.
c. 500,000 insects.
d. 100,000 insects.

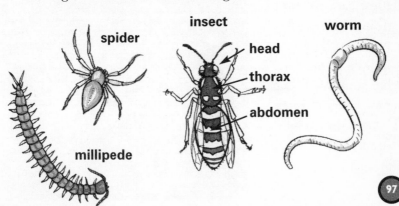

spider

insect

head

thorax

abdomen

worm

millipede

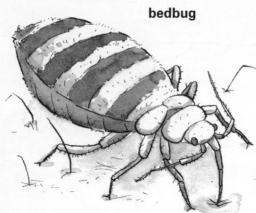

bedbug

The Skinny on Bugs:

If you want to get really technical, the only true bugs are those insects with beaklike mouthparts that can pierce and suck. Bedbugs, stinkbugs, aphids, treehoppers, and pond striders are among the true bugs.

From the Inside Out: Instead of bones, insects, spiders, centipedes, and millipedes have a hard outer covering called an *exoskeleton*. As a bug eats and gets bigger, it outgrows its exoskeleton. In this process, called *molting*, the exoskeleton splits down the middle like a pair of pants that are too tight. The bug then wriggles out (like the cicada at right is doing). It usually hides until its soft new exoskeleton hardens. Most bugs molt several times before they reach their full adult size and shape.

All Eyes Ahead: Adult insects have compound eyes that are made up of many individual eyes. Each little eye has six sides that fit with the others like a jigsaw puzzle. Having so many eyes allows an insect to detect movement from many directions at once. Though each eyelet sees

things separately, the insect's brain combines all the signals it receives to produce a complete image. Each one of a green darner dragonfly's compound eyes contains 28,000 eyelets—the most of any insect.

Seeing the Light:

Besides compound eyes, insects have another type of eye called the *ocellus*. This simple eye senses light but does not see images. Most adult insects have three ocelli, arranged in a triangle on the top of their head. The ocelli stimulate the

> ## Jeepers Creepers!
>
> One of the ways a cabbage white butterfly signals that she is looking for a mate is by covering her eye with . . .
>
> **a.** her eyelashes.
> **b.** a black lens.
> **c.** an eyelid.
> **d.** a wing.

insect to be more or less active depending on how much light there is. The brighter the light, the faster an insect will walk or fly. A housefly with its ocelli covered won't move at all.

Sun Block: Termites do not like strong light. A few species carry little umbrellas made from leaves when they first come up out of the ground.

Double Vision: The whirligig beetle's compound eyes are each divided into two separate parts so it can see both above and below the water as it spins around on the surface.

Jeepers Creepers!

The color of insect blood is . . .

a. deep purple or pink.
b. royal blue.
c. milky white.
d. clear or pale yellow or green.

The Better to Hear With: Some insects, such as the brush cricket, have ears on their legs.

Belly-Full: Locusts and some grasshoppers have ears on their abdomen.

Bug Sense: One way insects make sense of their world is through their antennae, which extend from a bug's head like wires. Though antennae are used mainly for smell and touch, some insects also use them to hear and taste.

Blood Drive:

A mosquito's antennae are very sensitive to heat. That's why mosquitoes are so good at locating warm-blooded victims to feast on, even in the dark.

Ant Scents: Ants produce chemicals that have distinctive odors. They can only tell each other apart by using their antennae to touch and smell each other.

Spider Sense: In place of antennae, spiders have *pedipalps*. Located on both sides of the head, pedipalps help spiders hear, feel, taste, and touch. Most web-making spiders have poor eyesight and are only able to tell when they have trapped an insect by the vibrations they feel through their palps. Pedipalps also make great little utensils for grabbing and holding prey during dinner.

Jeepers Creepers!

Which statement is true?

a. In some parts of Africa, children tie strings to goliath beetles and keep them as pets.
b. Using their powerful back legs, goliath beetles kick stones at predators.
c. Goliath beetles have the largest wingspan of any insect.
d. A goliath beetle will travel hundreds of miles to escape a dry spell.

Putting Out Feelers:

The antennae of the long-horned beetle can be as much as three times the length of its entire body.

Lightweight Champ: At about one-tenth of a millimeter long, the wingless male firefly wasp holds the record for smallest adult insect.

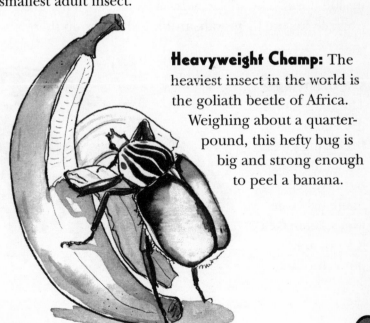

Heavyweight Champ: The heaviest insect in the world is the goliath beetle of Africa. Weighing about a quarter-pound, this hefty bug is big and strong enough to peel a banana.

Super Fly: Unlike most winged insects, the fly has only one pair of wings. In place of a second pair, it has two small knoblike structures that help keep it steady while in flight. But that doesn't stop flies from being the show-offs of the insect world. An appetizing-looking gnat on the ceiling can inspire a fly to flip itself over in midair and land upside down. The sticky pads on its feet are what make it possible for the fly to walk around while it's up there.

On the Wing:

The long "tail" at the end of each back wing gives the swallowtail butterfly its name. Its large wingspan makes it a fast and powerful flier.

Speed Dragons: One of the fastest fliers in the insect world, the dragonfly can reach speeds of over 30 miles per hour. Like most insects, it has two pairs of wings—one in front and one in back—that beat in opposite directions. As the front wings go up, the back wings go down.

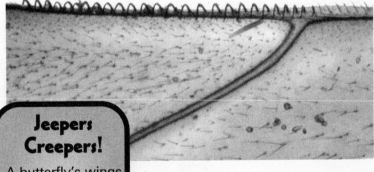

Jeepers Creepers!

A butterfly's wings are made up of . . .

a. scales that reflect light.
b. pigmented skin.
c. multicolored cells.
d. very fine hair.

In Sync: Like dragonflies, bees have two pairs of wings. But unlike the wings of the dragonfly, the bee's are connected by tiny hooks. These hooks guarantee that both sets of wings will beat together in the same direction when the bee flies.

Going the Distance:

Once the weather turns cold, the monarch butterflies of North America can no longer fly. That's why they head south in the winter, flying thousands of miles to find warmth. In fact, some butterflies travel all the way from Canada to Mexico. Scientists are not entirely sure how such tiny animals are able to fly such long distances. One reason may be that their bodies are quite small compared to their wings. Another may be that the butterflies conserve energy by coasting on currents of air. But perhaps the biggest mystery is how so many butterflies end up in the very same tree that they roosted in the year before!

Do-It-Yourself Surgery:

The Australian cockroach doesn't need wings because it lives underground. When it reaches maturity, it bites off its own wings.

Jeepers Creepers!

The fire beetle of Australia . . .

a. can walk through red-hot ashes.

b. gets its name from its bright scarlet coloring.

c. is used as a fire alarm because it buzzes loudly as soon as it smells smoke.

d. can start a fire by very quickly rubbing its back legs together.

Heat Seekers:

Like other insects, butterflies are cold-blooded and must get their energy to fly from solar heat. So when you see a butterfly resting on a leaf, its wings spread, soaking up the sun, it's actually warming up for the next flight.

Buzzing Off:
Mosquitoes, like other true flies, have only two wings. That annoying buzzing sound you hear when a mosquito circles your head is made by the extremely fast flapping of its wings—up to 600 times per second!

Hardly Flying:
Beetles such as ladybugs have hard front wings called *elytra*. The more delicate back wings are hidden underneath until the beetle is ready to fly. Then it opens its front wings and flaps its back wings. The extended front wings don't flap, but help the beetle rise up into the air.

Loopy Walks:

Some caterpillars have a funky way of moving. They grasp the ground tightly with their front legs and drag their back legs forward, scrunching up their middle in a loop. To straighten out, they reach forward with their front legs, leaving their back legs in place. Then they dig in and start all over again.

Wriggling Along: Worms are a farmer's friends. As they wriggle and squirm, tunneling from place to place underground, they break up and loosen the soil so that air can circulate. The mucous on their skin contains nitrogen, which helps plants grow. Worm castings—or worm poop—also contains nutrients that are good for plants. But if worms are so small, how is it they do a big farm so much good? It's because there are so many of them. Up to one million worms can be found in just one acre of land!

Jeepers Creepers!

Ribbon worms can grow to be 90 feet long and have been known to . . .

a. form bows as they slither on the ground.
b. tie themselves into knots.
c. get so tangled up with other ribbon worms that they can't tell where one worm ends and another begins.
d. travel at speeds of up to 30 miles per hour.

Making Tracks: Sporting one pair of legs for each segment of its flat-looking body, the centipede, also called a hundred-legger, can have from 15 to nearly 200 pairs. Six-legged insects move three legs at a time, two on one side and one on the other—a routine that gives them their zigzag motion. Centipedes can move swiftly, using the same basic gait but on a much grander scale.

Making Waves: Even though they are called thousand-leggers, millipedes only have about the same number of legs as centipedes. Unlike centipedes, however, millipedes have two pairs of short legs on each body segment, and their legs are

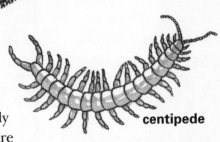

millipede

centipede

set below their rounded body rather than out to the side. Millipedes are slower than centipedes, and move ten or more pairs of legs at a time in a wavelike motion.

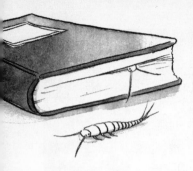

Bookworms? With no wings and a very flat body, the silverfish is perfectly suited for slithering into tight spaces. It's even been known to make itself at home between the pages of a book.

Flea for All: When it comes to jumping, fleas are the stars of the insect world. To jump as far as a flea, a person would have to jump the length of four football fields. The secret of the flea's amazing ability lies in a pad of *resilin*, a rubberlike material, above each of its heavily muscled back legs. As a flea gets ready to jump, it crouches, locking its hind legs against its body and tightly squeezing the resilin pads. When its legs snap free, the resilin releases the stored-up energy like a spring and catapults the flea high into the air.

Jeepers Creepers!

Which statement about scorpions is *not* true?

a. Scorpions can walk faster backward than they can forward.
b. Scorpions are weak fliers.
c. Scorpions often take off by jumping from a high elevation.
d. Scorpions have three sets of wings.

Step Right Up:

Imagine a circus in which all the participants are fleas. At one time, flea circuses were all the rage in Great Britain. A human ringmaster would use tweezers to lift the fleas, which were dressed in tiny clothing and harnessed by slender

silver wires, onto a tightrope or miniature stage where they would juggle and ride teensy little bikes.

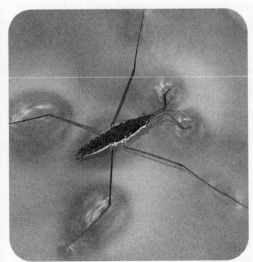

Skimming the Surface:

The water strider walks on water as easily as other bugs crawl on the ground. How does it do it? Molecules pulling on the surface of the water form a thin film. The water strider takes advantage of this by spreading its legs widely to support its weight evenly over the surface. Waterproof hairs on its legs also help keep it from breaking through the film.

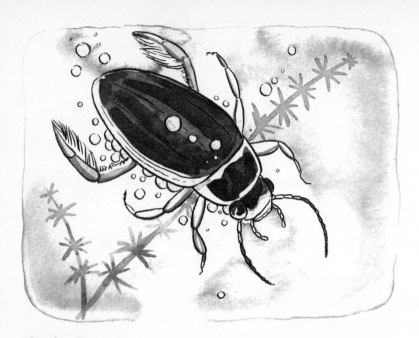

Scuba Bugs: The water beetle is able to spend most of its time underwater by storing air beneath its wings. The beetle breathes the air through tiny holes called *spiracles*. As the air supply is used up, the bubble acts like a kind of Aqua-Lung, taking in oxygen from the water.

Jeepers Creepers!

When the weather gets extremely hot, hopping grasshoppers cope by . . .

a. going for a swim.
b. moving along the ground at very high speeds.
c. growing a set of wings.
d. burrowing underground.

Ripley's Believe It or Not! Brain Buster

Drive yourself buggy with these brain-busting activities as you try to separate fact from fiction!

Robert Ripley dedicated his life to seeking out the bizarre and unusual. But every unbelievable thing he recorded was known to be true. In the Brain Busters at the end of every chapter, you'll play Ripley's role—trying to verify the fantastic facts presented. Each Ripley's Brain Buster contains a group of four shocking statements. But of these so-called "facts," **one** is **fiction**. Will you **Believe It!** or **Not!**?

Wait—there's more! Following the Brain Busters are special bonus games where you can play "Who am I?" by trying to **Name That Bug!** Finally, tally your score by flipping to the end of the book for answer keys and a scorecard.

Crawly creatures have the oddest features. But can you spot the one bogus bug characteristic below? Yes, one of these four facts is purely fiction—but which one? You'll get 20 points if you can figure it out.

a. Saw-toothed grain beetles have jagged-edged teeth that allow them to chew—what else?—grain.

Believe It!   **Not!**

b. Praying mantises can rotate their heads 180 degrees to look over their shoulders, allowing them to hunt for food quite effectively.

Believe It!   **Not!**

c. Fireflies, who use their "tail lights" to attract mates, are the only order of insects that can produce light.

Believe It!   **Not!**

d. A darkling beetle actually stands on its head to drink. After dew forms on its back in the morning, the beetle tips its head forward so the water droplets roll down its back and into its mouth.

Believe It!   **Not!**

BONUS GAME—NAME THAT BUG!

If you've ever been bitten by me, you know how annoying I can be. I am the stable pest, especially outside in the sunshine. You can usually find me flying around a certain galloping animal. Sometimes, I admit, I do bite humans. But believe me, I'd much rather be sucking the blood of my big four-legged buddies.

Who am I?

— — — — —   — — —

Bugs use sound, body language, and touch to communicate defensive, aggressive, or friendly behavior. But sometimes all they want to do is blend in.

Jeepers Creepers!

Some people think that if you count the number of chirps a cricket makes in 15 seconds and add 40, you can tell . . .

a. the air temperature.
b. the humidity.
c. how many hours until the next rainfall.
d. the number of stars you can see in the sky.

Love Songs: Bugs often attract mates with their songs. The male cicada uses a pair of special drumlike organs called *tymbals*. When the cicada contracts the muscles attached to the tymbals, they vibrate, producing the cicada's song. The song is amplified by a hollow section of the cicada's abdomen. Some cicadas can be heard for up to a quarter-mile away!

115

Food for Love: When he's ready to mate, a male scorpion fly catches a caterpillar, fly, or other juicy tidbit, then gives off a scent that will attract a female. When a female arrives, she inspects the male's gift—and it had better please her. Otherwise, she'll fly off in search of another mate who's caught something juicier.

Seeds of Love:

The male stinkbug sticks its pointed mouthparts into the kind of seed it likes to eat and holds it in place until a female stinkbug drops by. He gives her the seed and she lets him know that she appreciates his generosity by becoming his mate.

Dinner Dance: Worker bees have a special way of communicating. When one of them finds nectar, it goes home to the hive and spreads the news by doing a waggle dance. The speed of the waggle tells the others how far they have to fly to find the food, while the angle of the waggle tells them where to find it.

That's Using Their Heads: To warn their housemates that danger is near, soldier termites bang their heads against the floors and ceilings of their burrows. The sound echoes throughout the nest, sending the termites scurrying away to safety.

Jeepers Creepers!

Which statement is *not* true?

a. In some countries, people collect fireflies in net bags to wear around their ankles to light their way.

b. The light from two carbuncle beetles placed in a jar is bright enough to read by.

c. Firefly lanterns can be found in some gardens in Japan.

d. Spiders are afraid of fireflies.

Heads, I Win; Tails, I Win: The bulldog ant of Australia is one the fiercest types of ant. Once it takes a bite with its strong jaws, called *mandibles,* it never lets go. If you cut a bulldog ant in half, the front will grab its own tail with its teeth and the tail will sting the head. The fight can last for quite a long time.

The Terminator: The longest of all beetles, the Hercules beetle can measure up to eight inches long, horns included. When males fight, they use their horns to pick up the enemy and fling it away.

Double Whammy: The enemies of fire ants—including people—should think twice before bothering these fierce little bugs. They hold on to their victim with their jaws and sting repeatedly, injecting an extremely painful venom.

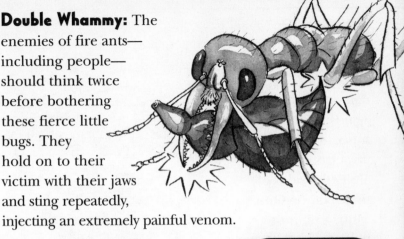

News Flash: Fireflies are really beetles. They talk to each other by flashing their lights. The male flashes first in midair. Several seconds later, the female, who is often wingless, answers from the ground with her own light. Each species of firefly has its own signal that is recognized by others of its species. But some fireflies mimic the signal of another species to lure and eat any unlucky prey that falls for the trick.

Jeepers Creepers!

To confuse predators, some grasshoppers are able to adjust the angle of their forewings to . . .

a. throw their voices like ventriloquists.
b. mimic praying mantises.
c. blend into the foliage.
d. create the impression that they have huge jaws.

Little Stinkers:

Millipedes are vegetarians. To defend themselves against hunters, they squeeze out stinking juice from pores along the sides of their bodies. One whiff, and most predators will scatter.

Beetle Juice: The bloody-nosed beetle can't fly. Nor can it run very fast. But it has one bizarre defense mechanism that explains its name. When danger lurks, the bloody-nosed beetle squeezes out a drop of bright

red liquid to discourage anything that wants to take a bite out of it. This stuff looks nasty and tastes even worse.

Ready, Set, Squirt! When under threat of attack, the wood ant points its abdomen toward its enemy. As the predator comes closer, the wood ant sprays it with acid from the tip of its abdomen.

Jeepers Creepers!

Desert beetles can kill other insects with their . . .

a. venom.
b. claws.
c. stingers.
d. odor.

Pain-Stalking: Centipedes are predators equipped with poison glands. A bite from a centipede can cripple its prey. Centipedes are not considered dangerous to humans, but the bite of some of the large tropical species can be very painful.

Playing Dead: The click beetle tries to escape notice by lying on its back, perfectly still. But if it's attacked, it snaps its head up, hurtling itself away from danger and landing on its feet. The beetle gets its name from the clicking noise it makes when it snaps its head.

CLICK!

Escape Artists:

Why do flyswatters have holes in them? Because the holes lessen the air pressure—which flies can detect via the hairs on their legs—thus giving you a better chance to surprise the fly and make a direct hit!

Presto Change-o!

The puss moth caterpillar is a master of disguise. Its green color helps it blend in with leaves. But if spotted, it can puff out a bright red fold of skin around its head, complete with spots that resemble two fierce-looking eyes. And if the predator comes closer, the caterpillar can stick out its tail and spray it with formic acid.

Black and Blue: The black grasshopper of Australia turns sky blue as soon as the sun comes up.

Smoke Screen: In 1850, natural history experts began to notice that the light-colored peppered moths that lived in industrial towns like Birmingham, England, had become darker in color. The scientists concluded that this

species of moth was forced to change, or *mutate*, along with its environment, which had become polluted with black soot. Moths in the countryside kept their original color.

Jeepers Creepers!

During the course of a summer, a katydid repeats its song about . . .

a. 50 million times.
b. 5,000 times.
c. 500,000 times.
d. 50,000 times.

Hiding in Plain Sight: Prey can barely see the cryptic tree bark spider when it rests on the tree bark it so closely resembles.

Heads or Tails? On each back wing, the hairstreak butterfly has markings that look a bit like a head and thin extensions that look like antennae. Predators have a hard time telling whether the butterfly is coming or going.

Nuts to You: The peanut bug has a hollow snout that looks like an unshelled peanut. If its head doesn't scare a predator away, the peanut bug opens it wings, revealing big red-and-black eye-shaped markings.

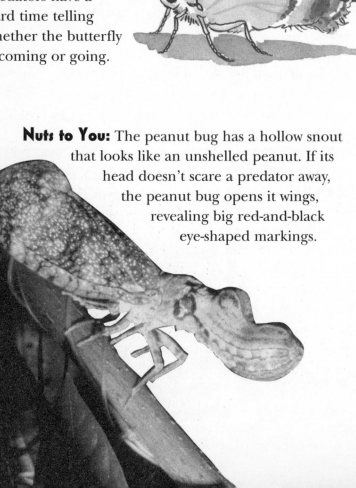

What a Hag!

For protection, the hag moth caterpillar doesn't just rely on looking like a dead leaf. It also has twisted black stinging hairs hidden among the brown hairs on its fleshy body.

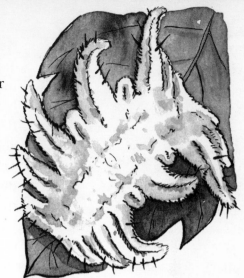

Hair-Raisers:

Fat, juicy caterpillars look yummy to most predators. But the hairs on their bodies make many caterpillars unfit for dinner. Some have hairs that are disgustingly sticky. Others have hairs or spines that are connected to poison glands and can even cause pain to humans. When touched, the spines of the puss caterpillar, for example, break off and release venom, causing swelling, a rash, and nausea.

Anti-Sonar Devices: Bats use a
form of sonar called *echolocation* to find the moths they love to eat. But some moths send out signals that are capable of jamming the bats' sound waves so that they can't determine the moths' locations.

Jeepers Creepers!

The male mole cricket's song is amplified by his burrow, and can be heard . . .

a. a half-mile away.
b. 100 feet away.
c. 1,000 feet away.
d. 50 yards away.

Hair Cuts:

Tarantulas that live in the Americas have barbed, bristlelike hairs on their abdomen called *urticating hairs*. When disturbed, they rub the hairs off with their back legs and send them flying at their attacker. If a small animal breathes in the hairs, its air passages may swell up so much that it suffocates.

Aphid Army: With their tiny, soft bodies, most aphids are pretty defenseless—except for the Alexander's horned aphid. Some members of this species have a hard, armorlike body and sharp, swordlike mouthparts. To defend themselves, they band together and attack a predator, holding on to it with their strong front legs while stabbing it with their mouthparts.

Bitter Beetles: When a predator notices the bright colors of ladybugs, it knows not to come near. Their striking coloration is a warning that these insects have a bitter taste and will make an attacker sick if it tries to eat them.

Jeepers Creepers!

To avoid being caught by bats, some moths . . .

a. play dead.
b. squirt venom.
c. fly backward.
d. chirp like birds.

Sticking Together: When predators come near, colonial caterpillars flip their bodies back and forth in a frantic frenzy. They stay so close to each other that the enemy thinks they are one big creature, and takes off in fright.

Built-in Survival Kit: With jaws strong enough to draw the blood of its enemies, and sharp, pointed spines, the spiny devil katydid is far from defenseless.

Roll Model: When threatened, the South African white lady spider doesn't stick around. Instead, it tucks in its legs and curls into a ball. Then away it rolls at breakneck speed, down sand dunes and far from predators.

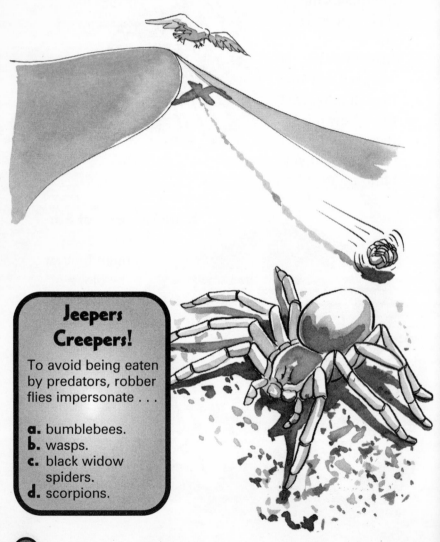

Jeepers Creepers!

To avoid being eaten by predators, robber flies impersonate . . .

a. bumblebees.
b. wasps.
c. black widow spiders.
d. scorpions.

You won't believe the bizarre names of certain bugs! But only three of the following incredible insects really exist. Can you find the phony?

a. The extraordinarily rare superfly got its name because of its super strength. Its muscle power rivals that of a small dog!
Believe It!   Not!

b. The confused flour beetle can be a pest of flourmills and grocery stores alike. (The "flour" part is clear, but what's the beetle so "confused" about?)
Believe It!   Not!

c. The acrobat ant looks like its doing a balancing act when it holds half its body up in the air.
Believe It!   Not!

d. The cucumber beetle loves to prey upon cucumbers in the garden.
Believe It!   Not!

BONUS GAME—NAME THAT BUG!

I am a hairy brown arachnid that looks pretty creepy.
Don't be fooled by my fast, aggressive movements—I am
really quite harmless. I don't spin webs like most of my
relatives. Instead, I hunt and capture my food. Though I
certainly can't make loud noises, I am named after a
mammal that howls.

Who am I?

_ _ _ _ _ _ _ _ _ _

Most bugs start out as eggs—and their parents have devised as many different ways to keep them safe as there are . . . well, bugs.

Jeepers Creepers!

Apple maggots produce chemicals that . . .

a. make their food tender enough to chew.
b. prevent a second female from laying eggs on fruit they already occupy.
c. keep birds away.
d. glue themselves to their perch.

Eggs-tremely Secure: Malacosoma moths lay strings of eggs that they wind around the limbs of fruit trees. The eggs are so tightly glued that the heaviest of storms cannot wash them away.

131

Eggs-tra Protection: A female cockroach lays hard little purselike cases. Inside each case are batches of eggs. When the wingless baby cockroaches, called *nymphs,* hatch, they look very much like their parents.

No Stalking Allowed:

Green lacewings lay each of their eggs at the end of a long, hairlike stalk. Out of reach, the eggs remain safe from small predators until hatching time.

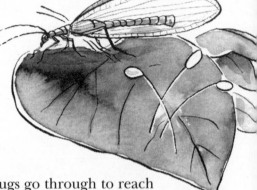

Heads Up: The process bugs go through to reach adulthood is called *metamorphosis.* Damselflies have three stages of metamorphosis: egg, nymph, and adult. The female damselfly lays her eggs below the surface of the water. To make sure she doesn't drown, the male holds on to her by the neck. After the eggs hatch, the young, or nymphs, live underwater until they become adults. They breathe through gills at the end of their tail.

Just a Stage: Many insects go through complete metamorphosis, which involves four stages. They start as eggs. When the young, called *larvae*, hatch, they do nothing but eat and grow. Moth larvae, for example, are caterpillars. To prepare for the third stage, *pupation*, the caterpillars produce a silk cocoon to wrap themselves in. While inside, the caterpillars develop into adults, and eventually emerge as moths.

Jeepers Creepers!

Some people believe that they can predict how long winter will last by finding a woolly caterpillar and measuring . . .

a. how long it is.
b. its weight.
c. the length of its brown middle.
d. how thick its "wool" is.

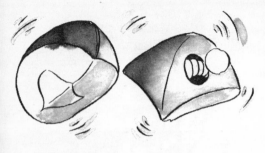

Mexican Jumping Bean: No, jumping beans don't really jump. After it hatches, the caterpillar of a small species of moth bores its way into the young seed of a bush. It eats the inside of the seed, then builds a web in the hollow shell. When the seed falls off the bush, the caterpillar flings itself from one side to the other, moving the bean and making it look as though it's jumping. The warmer the weather, the more the caterpillar moves around. When the caterpillar becomes a pupa, it stops moving. Months later, the adult moth chews a hole in the seed and flies away.

Deep Freeze: Cabbage butterflies spend winters in their pupa stage. A substance called *glycerol* in their body fluid acts as a kind of antifreeze, keeping the water inside the insect's cells from freezing and rupturing the cell membranes. Drops of glycerol seep through the cell walls so that ice forms outside the cells instead of inside. The glycerol causes the ice to form without jagged edges, giving added protection.

Jeepers Creepers!

The swallowtail caterpillar is usually left alone because of . . .

a. its bad taste.
b. its long, sticky tongue.
c. the hissing sound it makes.
d. the two large eyespots on its back.

From Grave to Cradle: At night, burying beetles use their remarkable sense of smell to locate newly dead birds, mice, and other small animals. If a male finds one, he sits on it and

either waits for a female to arrive or gives off a chemical to attract her. The two beetles then dig a hole under the corpse to bury it. Next, they strip the body of fur or feathers, roll it into a ball, and spray it with a fluid that helps preserve it. Finally, the female lays her eggs nearby. After hatching, the larvae, or grubs, can munch on the corpse or eat food that the parents throw up. Both parents stick around, keeping the corpse free of fungus and bacteria until the grubs are ready to pupate.

Hatchbacks: When a female giant water bug sees a male water bug that looks healthy and strong, she goes after him. After she catches him, she lays her eggs on his back, securing them with a special glue secreted from her body. The male water

bug has no choice but to carry the eggs around with him until they hatch.

Stock Pot: Each egg of the potter wasp gets its own little pot to protect it. The female wasp takes several hours to fashion a pot out of mud. Then she finds a juicy caterpillar, paralyzes it with her stinger, and stuffs it into the pot. Finally, she lays one egg in the pot and stops it up with more mud. Once the egg hatches, the larva has a caterpillar feast.

Playing Favorites: Scientists can't explain how, but potter wasp mothers know which eggs are male and which are female. For some reason, the males get smaller pots and less food than the females.

Dry Idea: Dragonflies lay their eggs in or near water. To keep from getting wet, these clever insects sometimes stand on water-lily pads while laying their eggs. Some dragonflies simply drop their eggs as they fly over the water. After the eggs hatch, the larvae may live underwater for several years.

Up, Up, and Away:

Some newly hatched spiders leave home by ballooning. First, they stand on tiptoe. Next, they spin a long silk line that drifts out behind them. Then, as soon as a breeze catches the strand of silk, they ride it until they land in a good spot to begin their new lives.

Pooper-Scoopers:

Like potter wasps, dung beetles go to a lot of trouble to protect their eggs. But instead of using mud, they scout out fresh mammal droppings and roll the dung into a ball. Then they poke a hole in the ball to lay their eggs in it. When the eggs hatch, the larvae have to eat through the dung to get out.

Jeepers Creepers!

In the first hour after a bee is born, it is fed . . .

a. hundreds of regurgitated worms.
b. watered-down honey.
c. crushed insects.
d. 500 times.

137

Mommy Dearest:

One kind of spider wasp
will do anything for
her offspring—even
attack a much
larger tarantula.
Though an adult
tarantula hawk wasp
eats nothing but
nectar, her larvae need
meat to grow. So before she lays an egg,
the mother wasp lures a tarantula out of its burrow and
paralyzes it with her poisonous stinger. Then she digs a
burrow, drags the spider inside, lays an egg on its
abdomen, and plugs up the hole. When the larva
hatches, its dinner is ready and waiting.

Hitching a Ride: Instead

of building a web, the
female wolf spider wraps her
eggs in a sac and carries
them around with her to
protect them. After they
hatch, the baby spiders live
on their mother's back until
they are old enough to hunt
on their own.

Full Cycle:

In early spring, aphid eggs hatch into wingless females that are already pregnant! Throughout the spring and summer, many generations of winged and wingless females are born, but it's not until fall that male aphids arrive. These winged males mate with wingless females, who lay the eggs that will hatch the following spring— and begin the cycle all over again.

Jeepers Creepers!

The largest land-dwelling animal on the continent of Antarctica is the . . .

a. polar bear.
b. wingless midge.
c. snow flea.
d. emperor penguin.

Eggs-tremely Protective:

Shield bugs are one of the very few types of insects that defend their eggs after they've laid them. If an enemy ventures too close to her nest, the mother will do her best to scare it away.

Blood Sisters: Male mosquitoes feed on flower nectar. Female mosquitoes feed on the blood of humans and other mammals. Without blood, a female mosquito's eggs will not develop.

Jeepers Creepers!

One type of insect lives in the ground for 17 years before reaching adulthood. Sometimes called the 17-year locust, it is really a . . .

a. great golden digger wasp.
b. desert-burrowing cockroach.
c. periodical cicada.
d. gladiator katydid.

Biting Story: Even though we say we have a mosquito "bite," we really don't. The mosquito doesn't bite, but pierces the skin with her long mouthpart, called a *proboscis,* then uses it to suck up the blood.

**What a cute baby! Err . . . maybe not. Bugs'
larval forms are unusual and distinct—but cute?
Not really. Of the following four curious bug baby
statements, can you spot the one that's just
kidding around?**

a. After mosquito larvae hatch in a pond, they collect
food by filtering water through their mouth. In a single
day, these tiny creatures can each filter about one liter
of water!

Believe It!   **Not!**

b. Acorn weevil larvae actually develop inside an acorn,
feeding on the nutmeat for about three weeks.

Believe It!   **Not!**

c. The scent of stinkbug nymphs is so powerful that
they are offended by their own stench. They try to wash
it off, but soon find out they are stuck with the smell
for life.

Believe It!   **Not!**

d. The larvae of Asian lady beetles, a type of ladybug,
are usually red and black and shaped like tiny
alligators.

Believe It!   **Not!**

BONUS QUESTION—NAME THAT BUG!

I am a true insect with a hard shell, and I live throughout North America. You can usually find me hovering around outdoor lights, particularly in the beginning of the summer. In fact, people got so used to seeing me then that they named me after the month in which summer begins.

Who am I?

— — — —   — — — — —

Plants, insects, fish, birds, even shoe polish—if it can be digested, chances are it will wind up on some bug's menu.

Spitting It Out: The spitting spider has silk glands connected to its venom glands. This night-hunter can't see very well, but it has long hairs on its front legs that help it sense when prey is near. Then it creeps up and spits out two streams of venomous silk in a zigzag pattern, immobilizing its unsuspecting victim.

Jeepers Creepers!

The saliva of leeches contains a substance called *hirudin* that is helpful to humans because it . . .

a. builds up red blood cells.
b. cures indigestion.
c. fights bacteria.
d. slows blood clotting.

Cave Cuisine:

The larvae of fungus gnats in New Zealand have a special way to attract their dinner. They hang out in caves, where they glow in the dark. But that's not all. The larvae spin silken threads, add sticky spit, and dangle the threads below them. As insects fly toward the light, they get caught in the threads. The larvae pull up their threads and have a feast. Yum!

Mouthwatering Experience:

Before it can eat, a housefly must turn its food into liquid. To do this, the fly spits digestive juices onto its food, then soaks up the liquid with spongelike pads on its proboscis. After the fly leaves, you can sometimes see the spots left by the dried-up juices.

Jeepers Creepers!

Dung beetles were used by the Ancient Egyptians . . .

a. to make scarab jewelry.
b. to make rattles for babies.
c. as live toys for their favorite cats.
d. as decorations for coffins.

Waste Not, Want Not:

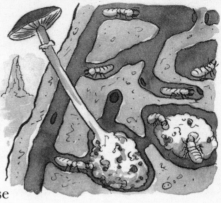

One kind of termite in Africa has gardens inside its mound. Worker termites grow a special kind of fungus in their own droppings. The fungus breaks down the undigested cellulose from the wood the termites eat. When the fungus— which is more easily digested than wood—is harvested, it's fed to the queen and king as well as the younger termites. As an added bonus, heat from the gardens helps keep air circulating through the mound.

Lip Service:

Unlike its parents, a dragonfly nymph lives underwater. It catches the tadpoles and small fish it likes to eat with a hinged lower lip operated by its own blood pressure. When the nymph isn't hunting, it folds and tucks its lip extension under its head and thorax. But as soon as something tasty swims by, watch out! In less than a second, out shoots the lip. Two pincers at the end snag the prey and pull it in for a tasty treat.

Gotcha! Instead of spinning a web, the trapdoor spider builds a burrow with, yes, a trapdoor. The burrow is about six inches deep. The trapdoor is made of dirt and is attached to the side of the burrow with silk that the spider spins. The spider camouflages the door with leaves, sticks, and small stones. Then it hides under the door, waiting for prey to come along. When the spider hears an insect on the other side, it jumps out, grabs the bug, and pulls it into the burrow.

Tongue in Cheek:

Hawk moths have extremely long, slender tongues that they keep tucked away until it's time to feed. Uncoiled, the hawk moth's tongue can  measure as long as 13 inches— perfect for reaching deep inside flowers to get the nectar they like to drink.

Forward . . . March!

South American army ants live in colonies of up to one million. The blind worker ants use their own bodies to form the nest, called a *bivouac*. When swarms of army ants are on the march, they eat all the bugs in their path—up to 100,000 in a single day. The worker ants are protected by soldier ants, which have such big jaws they can only eat if the workers feed them. In Africa, relatives of army ants are called driver ants. When they sweep through a village, everyone leaves. Inconvenient, perhaps, but after the driver ants move on, the people get to return to a bug-free village!

Buddy System:

Ants and aphids have a good thing going. The ants protect the aphids by eating the eggs of ladybugs and lacewings, whose larvae are aphid predators. Ants also let slow-going aphids hitch rides on their backs. To reward themselves, ants milk aphids to get the sugary honeydew they produce. When two different species cooperate in this way, it's called *symbiosis*.

Jeepers Creepers!

In 1479, the larvae of click beetles were tried and found guilty by the bishop of Lausanne, Switzerland, for the crime of . . .

a. carrying the plague.
b. eating stored grain.
c. devouring all the leaves on the trees.
d. eating all the crops.

Fungus Farm: Leaf-cutter ants have a well-developed system for producing their own food. First, worker ants cut off bits of leaves. Then smaller ants hop onto the leaves and guard against predators while the workers carry them back to the nest. The workers drop off the leaves at the entrance, where soldier ants with huge heads and fierce-looking jaws stand guard. Another group of worker ants carries the leaves underground, where they chew them up into a pulpy mass. This serves as a compost heap to grow the fungus that leaf-cutter ants need to thrive.

Web Sites: Many spiders spin webs to trap their prey. The webs are made from silk that the spider releases through tiny spigots called *spinnerets* on the back of its abdomen. The silk comes out as a liquid, but hardens as the spinnerets work like tiny fingers to weave the silk into the kind of web the particular spider weaves. Different types of webs include the orb web, the hammock web, the funnel web, and the sheet web.

It's a Wrap: Not all silk is used for webs. Spiders use different types of silk from different glands to protect their eggs, to make draglines so they can travel, and to hunt prey. Still another type of silk is used for storing food. If a spider is not going to eat its prey right away, it saves it by wrapping it up in hundreds of silken threads spun from its own special wrapping gland.

Target Practice: Orb webs look like beautifully constructed lace doilies and take about an hour to make. Since the webs are visible to insects, why don't they just fly around them? Scientists think that some webs may have the same kind of ultraviolet patterns that attract insects to flowers—which would explain why so many insects get caught in them!

149

Bungee Jumping Champion: When a jumping spider spots a potential meal, it attaches a silk dragline to its jumping-off point and leaps onto its prey. The dragline also serves as a lifeline in case the spider misses or needs to make a quick getaway. Some jumping spiders can leap 25 or more times their own body length.

In the Bag: The purse web spider spins itself a pouch of silk and stays inside waiting for an insect to land on it. Then it bites through the pouch to kill the unsuspecting bug before it knows what hit it.

Fast Food: The ogre-faced spider lives in tropical forests. At night, it hangs upside down just above the ground, holding a small sticky web with its four front legs. When a tasty morsel comes along, the spider hurls the web like a net to capture a midnight snack.

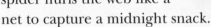

Jeepers Creepers!

Considered a sign of good luck, in some Middle Eastern countries spiders are . . .

a. placed in bassinets of newborn babies.
b. worn in the hair.
c. placed in the bed of newlywed couples.
d. given to children on their first day of school.

Armed and Dangerous: When they're not hiding from enemies by pretending to be bird droppings, bolas spiders have a unique way of hunting. They spin a silken thread with a glob of sticky stuff at one end. Holding onto the other end, they fling the thread to catch their prey and reel it in.

Vise Squad: Praying mantises count on the element of surprise. Great at blending in with its environment, a mantis balances on its back four legs and waits for prey to come near. Then, in a fraction of a second, it flicks out its barbed front legs and snaps them shut, holding its victim in a viselike grip. It's not uncommon for the mantis to eat another mantis, or to begin devouring its prey while it's still struggling to get away.

Sucking Up: The tear moth of Southeast Asia quenches its thirst in quite an unusual way. It lands and makes itself comfortable near the eye of a large mammal such as a buffalo. Then it inserts its long proboscis into the animal's eye and drinks its tears. The proboscis is so thin that it can slip under the eyelid of a sleeping animal without waking it up.

Jeepers Creepers!

Although it eats many different kinds of insects, a praying mantis will never eat . . .

a. a dragonfly.
b. a wasp.
c. an ant.
d. a bumblebee.

Thanks for Sharing:

Honey-pot ants live in desert areas and have an ingenious way to keep from starving when food is scarce. Storage ants called *repletes* are fed huge quantities of nectar. Barely able to move, they hang from the ceiling of the nest. If the repletes get too full, they will pop like little yellow balloons. But if the colony has trouble finding food, they need look no further than the storage ants. These obliging creatures will throw up all they have eaten so that the rest of the ants can have a meal.

Not Too Picky:

Cockroaches have been around for millions of years. Maybe it's because roaches will eat almost anything, from food scraps to cardboard to shoe polish to their own offspring. On the other hand, they can go for months without eating. If you cut off a roach's head, it can live for a week. The only reason it doesn't live longer is because it dies of thirst.

Liquid Lunch: The assassin bug hides and lies in wait for its prey. Then it strikes out with its beak, stabbing its victim and injecting it with venom. The chemicals dissolve the victim's insides so that they can be easily slurped up.

Fooling Around:

The ant-nest beetle lives among wood ants. The beetle tricks the ants into feeding it by giving off a chemical that makes it smell just like its hosts.

Jeepers Creepers!

Scientists can measure the amount of pollution in the atmosphere by . . .

a. studying bee pollen.
b. analyzing spider webs.
c. sifting through termite nests.
d. counting the flashes of fireflies.

Brain Buster

What's for dinner? If you're a bug, it could be just about anything. Can you tell which of these four gourmet bug stories has been cooked up just for you?

a. The wee harlequin beetle, a member of the stinkbug family, is known for its love of asparagus.
Believe It!   Not!

b. Talk about going hungry! Cecropia moths only live about two weeks because, in their adult form, they cannot eat. They don't even have a mouth or proboscis!
Believe It!   Not!

c. The antlion gets its name because, in its larval form, it loves to devour ants.
Believe It!   Not!

d. What picky eaters! When lurking in closets, moths actually prefer to chew on expensive designer clothes.
Believe It!   Not!

BONUS GAME—NAME THAT BUG!

I am a black-and-yellow striped beetle that lives primarily in western regions of North America. My name comes from the food I eat—I am a vegetable-crop pest that loves to feed on the plant of a certain brown, round, under-the-ground vegetable.

Who am I?

— — — — — — — — —

5 Bug Abodes

Insect homes come in all shapes and sizes, from the simplest leaf to the most complex underground burrow.

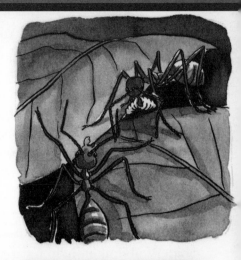

Child Labor: Tailor ants, also known as weaver ants, make their nests in the leaves of trees. While some worker ants pull the edges of the leaves together, others move along, each holding an ant larva in its jaws and squeezing until the larva releases a bit of the same silk it will later use to build its cocoon. As the sticky silk dries, it glues the leaves tightly together.

Jeepers Creepers!

Leaf-cutter ants are such great escape artists that zookeepers have to . . .

a. coat the walls of their glass cages with slippery chemicals.
b. make their cages out of the finest iron mesh.
c. surround their cages with poisonous snakes.
d. cover their feet with Vaseline.

Construction Paper:

Like bees, social wasps live and work within a group. To build their nests, they make a paperlike substance by chewing on wood fibers. You've probably seen the large, gray, egg-shaped nests of the North American bald-faced hornets (which are really wasps) hanging from a tree branch or under the eaves of a building. Try looking at the nest with binoculars and see if you can spot streaks of color. If the wasps chewed on wood that was painted, their nest will be streaked with whatever color was on the wood!

Bug in a Bubble: The water spider spins its underwater nest from silk, then stocks it with air. Tiny hairs on the spider's abdomen help it carry air bubbles down from the surface. After it traps enough air under the silk, it settles down to wait for prey. When something tasty happens along, the water spider attacks and brings its meal back into its comfy, air-filled web to eat.

Astounding Mounds: It takes the fungus-growing termites that live in the tropical grasslands of Africa years to construct their homes, which can reach 20 feet high. These towers, built out of saliva and either sand, clay, or sawdust, feature elaborate networks of interlacing tunnels. At the center of each mound are fungus gardens, and hidden deep within is the royal chamber, home to the king and queen. The queen may lay up to 30,000 eggs a day, providing enough soldier and worker termites to keep the whole operation running smoothly.

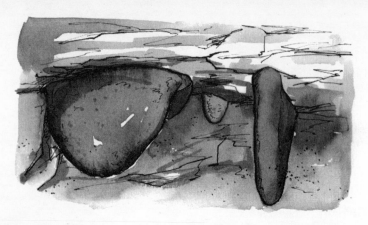

Bee-hemoth: Under cliffs in the Himalayan Mountains, giant honeybees build honeycombs that measure up to seven feet long and weigh up to 400 pounds.

Keeping Their Cool: Bees build hives of wax consisting of individual six-sided cells. The wax is produced by the bees themselves. In extreme heat, bees have several ways to air-condition their hive. One way is to beat their wings like fans, sending currents of air throughout the hive. Another way is to plug up openings in empty cells with water or diluted honey. As the liquid evaporates, it cools the air.

Hide-and-Seek: The nymphs of froghopper bugs—also called spittlebugs—love to eat plant sap. But most plants are teaming with predators that love to eat froghopper nymphs! The solution? The nymphs cover themselves with

frothy bubbles that look like spit. The froth consists of air mixed with liquids that are secreted from the nymphs' rear end and abdomen.

Petal Palace: In Central and South America, some ants carry seeds into their nest. In time, they sprout, making the nest look like a tiny flower garden.

Jeepers Creepers!

In a beehive, there can never be more than one queen. When the old queen dies, the new queen emerges from her cocoon and . . .

a. seals the door of her cell with a special glue.
b. stabs her sisters to death with her stinger.
c. immediately lays 5,000 eggs.
d. drinks all the honey.

Tomb and Gloom: Bees are far from hospitable to uninvited guests. If a creature such as a mouse accidentally drops by the hive, the bees band together and sting it to death. Then they go outside and gather sticky material that can be found on plants and twigs. They use the sticky stuff to bind the corpse like a mummy. When it dries and hardens, the intruder is left where it died, entombed in the hive.

Mobile Home:
The caddis fly larva lives underwater in a tube-shaped mobile home it builds for itself. It uses sand and bits of leaves and sticks, which it glues together with spit. Only the larva's head is visible, peering out from one end as it creeps along the bottom of the pond.

Bag It: The Colletes bee makes an underground nest with a tiny cell for each of her eggs. To protect them, she lines the cells with a polyester-like substance she excretes from a special gland. Then she fills the cells with food for the

larvae to eat when they hatch. Scientists who have analyzed the substance have found that, although it is not woven, it is essentially the same as the manufactured polyester used in clothing.

Mini Apartment Houses: The female carpenter bee drills a tunnel a little less than a foot long inside a broken twig—quite a feat for such a tiny creature. To equal the effort, a human would have to dig a hole 200 feet deep by hand. The bee

lines the inside of her tunnel with several pollen-filled layers, separated from each other by a partition. Each little apartment contains one egg. When the eggs hatch, the baby bees eat the pollen and chew their way to freedom.

Jeepers Creepers!

A type of European bee makes its nest in the empty shells of . . .

a. crayfish.
b. bird eggs.
c. snails.
d. turtles.

On a Roll:

Leaf-rolling weevils and their distinctive nests, which hang from trees like miniature, green-colored egg rolls can be found throughout the world. These tiny beetles cut leaves in precise ways to make their nests. The weevil notches each side of a leaf

near the stem from the outside edge to the middle. As soon as the leaf wilts, the weevil presses the two sides together. Then, starting from the tip, the weevil rolls the leaf back toward its body, makes a slit, and lays its egg inside. After sealing in the egg, the weevil finishes rolling the leaf up. When the larva hatches, it gets out by eating its way through the layers of leaf.

Hives, holes, and nests . . . there are all kinds of places that bugs call home. But don't let these four homey details deceive you. One of these bug abodes is bogus.

a. Earwigs can survive in any crevice or small space, but they prefer to live in certain animals' ear canals.
Believe It!   Not!

b. Pecans are in serious danger when shuckworms are around. This worm tunnels in and makes its home inside the nut, preventing it from developing properly.
Believe It!   Not!

c. The cigarette beetle often makes its home in tobacco farms and manufacturing facilities, since it likes to feed on dried, stored tobacco.
Believe It!   Not!

d. One super colony of ants in Japan spanned an area of about 1.7 miles. The colony is reported to have had more than one million queens and more than 300 million worker ants.
Believe It!   Not!

BONUS GAME—NAME THAT BUG!

I am commonly mistaken for a spider, but I am really a close relative known as a harvestman. My legs are thinner and longer than a spider's, and I only have one body section instead of two. People often think I'm poisonous and get scared when they find me in their basement. But the truth is, I am totally harmless. In fact, there's something *parental* about me . . .

Who am I?

_ _ _ _ _ _   _ _ _ _ _ _ _ _

POP QUIZ

This section is crawling with score-builders—it's time for the official Pest Test! Have you caught all the bizarre bug facts in this book? Well, investigate your insect insight with this quiz. Pencils ready?

1. Which of the following is *not* a true bug?
a. Aphid
b. Treehopper
c. Pondstrider
d. Maggot

2. Molting occurs when . . .
a. a bug outgrows its exoskeleton.
b. tree bark peels off after certain bug infestations.
c. a bug starts eating its way out of a cocoon.
d. termites invade a building.

3. Insect antennae are *not* used to . . .
a. see.
b. smell.
c. hear.
d. sense temperature.

4. The Australian cockroach bites off its antennae when it reaches full maturity.
       Believe It!   **Not!**

5. Which of the following buggy-love stories is *not* true?

a. Scorpion flies woo their mates with insect gifts.

b. Cicadas use drumlike organs to sing to their honeys.

c. Female graffiti bugs attract a mate's attention by carving symbols into wooden porches and steps.

d. Female water bugs mate with big strong hunks—then let them carry the fertilized eggs on their back.

6. Some insects taste foul in order to discourage predators from attacking. Can you spot the insect that makes a particularly sickening snack?

a. Ladybug

b. Cricket

c. Stinkbug

d. Termite

7. When an insect undergoes complete metamorphosis, it passes through four stages. What is the correct order?

a. Egg, larva, pupa, adult.

b. Larva, egg, pupa, adult.

c. Pupa, adult, egg, larva.

d. Egg, larva, adult, pupa.

8. Some insects protect their eggs by wrapping them up. Can you tell which one of these three statements is egg-straordinarily *un*true?

a. Dung beetles lay their eggs in balls of dung.

b. Wolf spiders carry their eggs around with them, safe inside a sac.

c. Purse ants weave tiny purses out of grass to keep their eggs safe.

d. Potter wasps lay their eggs in tiny mud pots.

9. A certain kind of moth actually drinks tears from a sleeping animal's eyes.

Believe It!   **Not!**

10. A housefly eats its meals in which of the following amazing methods?
a. By smashing the food between its wings.
b. By decomposing the food in a covering of fungus.
c. By landing upon the food and sucking it up through its hollow legs.
d. By liquefying the food with spit.

11. Spiders use their silk in all kinds of cool ways. But one of these four uses is nothing but a yarn. Can you spot it?
a. Storing food
b. Communicating
c. Traveling
d. Protecting their eggs

12. A cockroach can live for a week without its head. Eventually, it dies because of . . .
a. dehydration.
b. starvation.
c. coldness.
d. boredom.

13. Some wasps regurgitate wood fibers to build their nests, which can have brightly colored streaks if the wasp has been chewing on painted wood.

Believe It!   **Not!**

14. Fungus-growing termites in Africa construct homes that can be as tall as . . .

a. 5 feet.
b. 10 feet.
c. 15 feet.
d. 20 feet.

15. Three of the following bee statements are buzzing with truth. Which one is pure make *bee*-lieve?

a. Bees may kill and entomb uninvited guests who enter the hive.
b. Bee babies spend their first 12 hours living underwater.
c. Bees may keep the hive cool by beating their wings to act as fans.
d. Giant honeybees have built hives that weigh as much as 400 pounds.

Answer Key

Chapter 1

Creature Features

Page 97:   **b.** 200 million insects.

Page 99:   **b.** a black lens.

Page 100:   **d.** clear or pale yellow or green.

Page 102:   **a.** In some parts of Africa, children tie strings to goliath beetles and keep them as pets.

Page 105:   **a.** scales that reflect light.

Page 106:   **a.** can walk through red-hot ashes.

Page 108:   **b.** tie themselves into knots.

Page 110:   **d.** Scorpions have three sets of wings.

Page 112:   **c.** growing a set of wings.

Brain Buster: c. is false.

Bonus Game: horse fly

Chapter 2

Going Buggy

Page 115:   **a.** the air temperature.

Page 117:   **d.** Spiders are afraid of fireflies.

Page 119:   **a.** throw their voices like ventriloquists.

Page 121:   **d.** odor.

Page 123:   **a.** 50 million times.

Page 125:   **a.** a half-mile away.

Page 126:   **a.** play dead.

Page 128:   **a.** bumblebees.

Brain Buster: a. is false.

Bonus Game: wolf spider

Chapter 3
Bug Babies
Page 131:   **b.** prevent a second female from laying eggs on fruit they already occupy.

Page 133:   **c.** the length of its brown middle.

Page 134:   **d.** the two large eyespots on its back.

Page 137:   **d.** 500 times.

Page 139:   **b.** wingless midge.

Page 140:   **c.** periodical cicada.

Brain Buster: **c.** is false.

Bonus Game: June beetle

Chapter 4
Bug Buffet
Page 143:   **d.** slows blood clotting.

Page 144:   **a.** to make scarab jewelry.

Page 147:   **d.** eating all the crops.

Page 149:   **b.** caterpillar cocoon.

Page 151:   **c.** placed in the bed of newlywed couples.

Page 152:   **c.** an ant.

Page 154:   **a.** studying bee pollen.

Brain Buster: **d.** is false.

Bonus Game: potato bug

Chapter 5
Bug Abodes
Page 157: **a.** coat the walls of their glass cages with slippery chemicals.

Page 159: **a.** for more than 4,000 years.

Page 161: **b.** stabs her sisters to death with her stinger.

Page 163: **c.** snails.

Page 164: **b.** air-conditioned by a series of tunnels.

Brain Buster: **a.** is false.

Bonus Game: daddy longlegs

Pop Quiz

1. **d.**
2. **a.**
3. **a.**
4. **Not!**
5. **c.**
6. **a.**
7. **a.**
8. **c.**
9. **Believe It!**
10. **d.**
11. **b.**
12. **a.**
13. **Believe It!**
14. **d.**
15. **b.**

What's Your Ripley's Rank?

Ripley's Scorecard

Well done! Your brain is a-buzzing with unbelievable bug facts! Now it's time to tally up your answers and get your Ripley's rating. Have you got **Insect Insight**? Or maybe you're **Bugging Out**? Add up your scores to find out!

Here's the scoring breakdown. Give yourself:
★ **10 points** for every **Jeepers Creepers!** you answered correctly;
★ **20 points** for every fiction you spotted in the **Ripley's Brain Busters**;
★ **10 points** for every time you were able to **Name That Bug!**;
★ and **5** for every **Pop Quiz** question you got right.

Here's a tally sheet:
Number of **Jeepers Creepers!**
questions answered correctly: _____ x 10 = _____

Number of **Ripley's Brain Buster**
fictions spotted: _____ x 20 = _____

Number of **Name That Bug!**
riddles solved: _____ x 10 = _____

Number of **Pop Quiz** questions
answered correctly: _____ x 5 = _____

Total the right column for your final score: _____

0-100
Something's buzzing . . .

. . . and it's the bug world. You know, those little crawly things you might have noticed all around you? Okay, so bugs aren't really your thing. That's all right. There are lots of other strange and unusual Ripley's facts to bug out about. Why not pick up some other zany Ripley books like *World's Weirdest Gadgets* or *Odd-inary People*?

101-250
Insect Insight

You're starting to get the bug! The unbelievable world of insects is luring you in slowly but surely. Don't be shy! Stand up and shout it loud and clear that the bug world is the best! All those amazing abilities and unlikely talents . . . just thinking about it is enough to make your head buzz. So many bugs, so little time to learn about them all!

251-400
Crawling with Knowledge

You've got this bug thing down! Your brain is crawling with all kinds of insect smarts—and you're not afraid to use 'em. Not only have you got a sense for the strange, you are perceptive in telling the difference between phony facts and remarkable realities. You might miss one here and there, but hey, nobody's perfect, right? Keep up the creepy-crawly curiosity.

401-575
Bugging Out!

Yep, you've definitely been bitten. You know more about the insect kingdom than may be good for you. (Unless of course, you plan on becoming an entomologist!) Eight-inch-long beetles, one million–member ant colonies, and poisonous silk-spitting spiders—this stuff is no big deal to *you*. And to top it all off, you've got a great eye for separating fact from fiction. Robert Ripley would be proud, even if your family might be a bit freaked out.

Believe It!®

Photo Credits

Ripley Entertainment Inc. and the editors of this book wish to thank the following photographers, agents, and other individuals for permission to use and reprint the following photographs in this book. Any photographs included in this book that are not acknowledged below are property of the Ripley Archives. Great effort has been made to obtain permission from the owners of all materials included in this book. Any errors that may have been made are unintentional and will gladly be corrected in future printings if notice is sent to Ripley Entertainment Inc., 5728 Major Boulevard, Orlando, Florida 32819.

Blasts
from the
Past

Contents

Introduction

Ripley Takes on the Past

The past is filled with little-known facts that you probably won't find in your history books. These are the kind of facts that fascinated Robert Ripley, creator of Believe It or Not! The first cartoonist to become a millionaire, Ripley liked to illustrate historical facts that would surprise, shock, or amuse his readers. To Ripley,  the fact that George Washington had lost all but one tooth by his mid-fifties and had six sets of dentures was far more interesting than conventional facts such as where or when Washington was born.

Perhaps Ripley's fascination with the most remarkable aspects of history is one reason why he made sure that the hours and days of his own life were so memorable.

An avid traveler, Ripley visited 201 countries during his lifetime. He loved to explore out-of-the-way places, making grueling treks into remote regions, often on the back of a donkey or a camel.

One place Ripley could not get enough of was China. Charmed by its sheer antiquity, he returned again and

again. The tombs of the Ming Dynasty (1368–1644) filled Ripley with awe, as did the larger-than-life-sized carved stone animals and warriors surrounding them. Because elephants are not native to China, the stone elephants are evidence of contact between China and Thailand at the time the tombs were built. This was the way that Ripley liked to learn about history—with three-dimensional clues that brought the past to life for him.

The Ripley archives are filled with quirky stories from the past featuring famous characters whose behavior was more than a little offbeat—people like King George II, who was saved from enemy soldiers by a loyalist who hid him beneath her hoop skirt, or the Earl of Derby, whose dying wish was that two roosters be brought to his sickroom so that he could watch them fight.

Ripley assured his own place in history when he declared in a 1929 cartoon: "America Has No National Anthem." After the cartoon appeared, enormous public demand led to Congress declaring "The Star-Spangled Banner" the official national anthem just over a year later.

OF ANACREON IN TWINE -
WE MYRTLE OF VENUS
WITH BACCHUS'S VINE"

AMERICA HAS NO NATIONAL ANTHEM

THE U.S.A. (BEING A DRY COUNTRY) HAS BEEN USING WITHOUT AUTHORIZATION — A VULGAR OLD ENGLISH DRINKING SONG AS RECENT AS 1914 CONGRESS REFUSED TO ENDORSE THE "STAR SPANGLED BANNER" WHICH IS THE AIR OF "TO ANACREON IN HEAVEN"

Think history's a bore? *Blasts from the Past* is filled with stories like these that just might change your mind. See how much you already know about the past by taking the One for the Books! quizzes and the Ripley's Brain Buster in each chapter. Then try your hand at the Pop Quiz at the end of the book and figure out your Ripley's rank with the handy scorecard.

Remember—Robert Ripley made history. Maybe you can, too!

Believe It!®

The mysteries of the past are solved by detectives called archaeologists, who use shovels, picks, chisels, and *lots* of brainpower.

One for the Books!

Picture-writing dating back to the caveman era was found above the entrance to a cave. Roughly translated, the message said which of the following?

a. Welcome!
b. Please wipe your feet.
c. Keep out!
d. Beware of bats.

Old As Dirt: In 1952, 13-year-old Donald Baldwin discovered a 5,000-year-old burial ground in Oconto, Wisconsin. It belonged to the Copper Culture people, who were one of the first in the world to make forged copper tools such as the awls, spear points, and fish hooks that were found at the site.

Long Live the King:

In ancient times, civilization thrived in Mesopotamia, a fertile area between the Tigris and Euphrates rivers that is now part of Iraq. Every New Year—or whenever the omens were very bad—the people of Mesopotamia sacrificed the life of their king to please the gods. Actually, the real king took the day off and some other poor soul was chosen to be king for the day. In 1861 B.C.E., Enlil-Bani was the king's stand-in. Just as the noose was about to be placed around his neck, an unbelievable thing happened. A messenger rushed in with news that the real king had just died. Enlil-Bani was spared and went on to rule the kingdom for 24 years.

Hard to Swallow:

Archaeologists in Sweden discovered the world's oldest chewing gum—a 9,000-year-old piece of birch resin with teeth marks in it.

One for the Books!

When the grave of a Neanderthal man buried 60,000 years ago was opened, it was found to contain . . .

a. a pet monkey.
b. flowers.
c. a necklace made from a mammoth tusk.
d. a portrait of a loved one.

Tall Story: Mysterious burial mounds found across the United States must have been built by a prehistoric race of giants. All the skeletons of adults found beneath the mounds were seven to eight feet long.

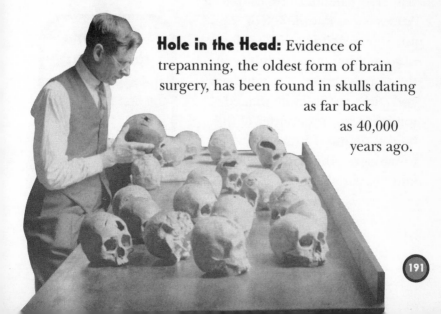

Hole in the Head: Evidence of trepanning, the oldest form of brain surgery, has been found in skulls dating as far back as 40,000 years ago.

191

Sharp-Tongued:

Robert Ripley traveled to Mexico City, where he posed with the Aztec Calendar Stone. Unearthed in 1760, the stone is nearly 12 feet wide and weighs more than 20 tons. Its carvings record what the Aztecs believed were the first four epochs of the world and show the 18 months of the Aztec year. The calendar reveals that the Aztecs had a knowledge of astronomy, but it is also evidence of something more primitive. At the stone's center, the Aztec sun god sticks out its knife-shaped tongue, a grim reminder of the food it required from its worshipers—human blood and hearts.

One for the Books!

The Aztecs were the first to . . .

a. put candles on birthday cakes.
b. create cartoons with speech balloons.
c. play table tennis.
d. make rock candy.

Busybody: Over the course of his lifetime, Pliny the Elder (23–79 C.E.) was governor of Germany, Gaul, Spain, and Africa, as well as both a general and an admiral in the armed forces of ancient Rome. During this time, he wrote a 37-volume encyclopedia of natural history, a 31-volume history of Rome, a 20-volume history of Roman warfare, a six-volume manual of public speaking, and eight books

of Latin grammar. When Mount Vesuvius erupted, Pliny sailed toward Herculanium instead of away from it, taking notes all the while. His notes survived the disaster, but, sadly, Pliny did not.

Same Old, Same Old: Archaeologists excavating Roman ruins along Hadrian's wall in northern England have unearthed clothing, shoes, letters, tax records—even a 2,000-year-old invitation to a birthday celebration that includes the first known sample of a woman's handwriting in Latin.

193

Breaking the News: In ancient times, scribes were often the only people who could read and write. Fearing that scribes would write bad things about them, the rulers of invading armies made sure to round them up before anyone else. In ancient Maya, for example, conquering rulers ensured that their prisoners' writing days were over by having their fingers broken and their fingernails torn out!

Taking Notes: It's been known for a while that the ancient Sumerians of Mesopotamia kept written records on clay tablets as long ago as 3300 B.C.E. But scientists have recently discovered that they kept track of merchandise on small clay *tokens* as much as 5,000 years earlier!

One for the Books!

An amazing find provided a clue that life can exist even inside a 4,000-year-old Egyptian mummy case. What was it?

a. Dormant dragonfly larvae.
b. A seed from which flowers were subsequently grown.
c. New hair growth on the mummy.
d. Cockroach eggs that hatched after the coffin was opened.

Picture This: In ancient Egypt, a system of picture-writing called hieroglyphics was used until about 400 C.E. So how is it that scholars are able to translate a form of writing that died out over 1,600 years ago? A stone tablet called the Rosetta Stone is the answer. Discovered in Egypt in 1799, the stone has three different scripts carved into it: Greek, Egyptian hieroglyphics, and demotic, a late form of Egyptian writing.

The easily translated Greek served as a key for deciphering the hieroglyphics. What does the writing say? Lots of good things about the ruling pharaoh, of course. Seems the scribe who wrote it was playing it safe!

Holy Smoke: To enter certain ancient Greek and Egyptian temples, you had to know the secret. Mysterious hidden doors would open only when a fire was lit on a special altar outside.

Breaking the Rules: When her husband, the pharaoh, died, Hatshepsut was supposed to rule until her son was old enough to take the throne. But she liked her job so much that she declared herself pharaoh and appeared before her subjects wearing a phony beard—because beards

were a symbol of power. Hatshepsut's reign extended from 1503 to 1482 B.C.E., breaking the 2,000-year-tradition of male-only rule. Unlike the pharaohs before her, she was devoted to peace and prosperity and opposed to waging war.

Under Wraps: To make a mummy, Egyptian embalmers used 400 pounds of natron salt (sodium carbonate) and 150 yards of linen strips.

Mummy's Day:

In 1996, a temple guard in Egypt discovered the largest number of mummies ever found in one place—and he wasn't even looking for them! The donkey he was riding got its hoof stuck in what the guard thought was a small pothole. As he gently removed the donkey's hoof, he peered through the hole

and saw many amazingly well-preserved mummies covered with gold. Archaeologists estimate that there are 10,000 bodies in the two square miles of what is now known as the Valley of the Golden Mummies. Though some of them wear gold masks, others wear carved masks painted with lifelike portraits. One mummy sports rows of carved red curls beneath her crown.

One for the Books!

To cure a sick baby, mothers in ancient Egypt would sometimes eat a . . .

a. scarab beetle.
b. camel's eye.
c. mouse.
d. raw ostrich egg.

Anybody Home?

Archaeologists digging under the leaning tower of Pisa in 1992 discovered an ancient Roman house. Complete with furniture and dinner plates, the house was less than three feet below ground level.

A Mammoth Job: Taller at the shoulder than a double-decker bus, the mammoth was one of the largest land mammals that ever lived. Neanderthal men and women ate its meat, wore its skin, and used its oily bones to keep their fires burning and its tusks to fasten roofs to their dwellings. How did hunters slay these huge beasts? With nothing more than rocks and flint-tipped wooden spears!

Lighting the Way: An ingenious lighting system was discovered in a series of caves in Hal Saflieni Hypogeum on the island of Malta. Constructed 5,000 years ago, the highly polished stone walls enabled a single ray of sunlight to illuminate the entire labyrinth.

Rolling Stones: The first taxicab in history was unearthed by archaeologists in Rome. The 2,000-year-old horse-drawn carriage was equipped with a meter that dropped pebbles into a drum when a rear wheel revolved. Counting the pebbles determined the amount of the fare.

One for the Books!

To ensure the privacy of ancient stone writings, the very first envelopes were made out of . . .

a. mammoth skin.
b. mud.
c. dung.
d. wax.

Ceiled Fate: Anastasius I (c. 430–518 C.E.), emperor of Byzantium, was warned that he would be killed by lightning. No doubt that is why he always ran for shelter at the slightest hint of a storm. One stormy day, Anastasius ran into an old house to avoid the lightning. Big mistake! The ceiling came crashing down and crushed him to death.

Boar Lore: According to legend, Diocletian (c. 245–313 C.E.) was told by a prophet that he would become emperor of Rome by killing a wild boar. After he learned to hunt, he killed lots of wild boars. But it was not until he stabbed the assassin of Emperor Numerian to death that

Diocletian was crowned emperor of Rome. What did the assassin's name mean in Latin? Wild Boar.

Faces of the Past: Easter Island, about 2,000 miles west of South America, is known throughout the world for the gigantic statues called Moai that dot the island. Created about 700 years ago by a lost culture, these eerie disembodied heads stand an average of 20 feet tall and weigh about 18 tons. Stone tools were used to carve the statues from the rock in the crater of an extinct volcano. Then the islanders moved the statues up to 14 miles away to stone platforms, called *ahu*—even though the islanders had no horses or oxen to pull them. How? No one really knows.

One for the Books!

If the age of Earth were represented by a 12-hour clock, the entire written history of humanity would represent . . .

a. four hours.
b. fifteen minutes.
c. one hour.
d. eight seconds.

Sometimes truth really is stranger than fiction. And now it's your turn to tell the difference in these out-of-the-ordinary activities!

Robert Ripley dedicated his life to seeking out the bizarre and unusual. But every unbelievable thing he recorded was known to be true. In the Brain Busters at the end of every chapter, you'll play Ripley's role—trying to verify the fantastic facts presented. Each Ripley's Brain Buster contains a group of four shocking statements. But of these so-called "facts," **one** is **fiction**. Will you **Believe It!** or **Not!**?

Wait—there's more! Following the Brain Busters are special bonus games in which you'll try to solve a tricky "History Mystery." To see how you rate, flip to the end of the book for answer keys and a scorecard.

Ancient arti-fact or fiction? Of the following four fantastic facts, one is pure fantasy. Can you unearth the one imposter?

a. Danish astronomer Tycho Brahe spent much of his life with a fake nose made of gold and silver.

Believe It!   **Not!**

b. In 1984, archaeologist Rachel Jordan excavated what scientists believe is a prehistoric baseball field. Jordan's work suggests that a primitive type of the game may have been played by Neanderthals.

Believe It!   **Not!**

c. An old wooden bridge spanned Kangaroo Valley in New South Wales, Australia, for nearly 100 years. On February 8, 1898, it was replaced by a modern suspension bridge. Six days later, the old bridge was destroyed by a flood.

Believe It!   **Not!**

d. A finger of ancient astronomer Galileo Galilei is on display at the Institute and Museum of the History of Science in Florence, Italy.

Believe It!   **Not!**

BONUS GAME—HISTORY MYSTERY

A certain transformation in 1918 shifted the way that Americans considered their days and time in general. One day, it was declared that the sun would set later. And people had to get out of bed earlier! This sudden change is still in effect today. What happened in the United States in 1918 to change people's days so drastically?

Maybe, but on closer inspection, it seems some days were good, some were weird, and others were downright disgusting!

Digest This! During the Middle Ages, 20 years of chopping off people's heads qualified executioners to become doctors. But in order to practice medicine, a physician had to know Latin. Since most executioners were not bilingual, some of them swallowed the pages of Latin dictionaries in the hopes that it would help them become fluent in the language!

One for the Books!

Catherine the Great of Russia suffered a fatal stroke while . . .

a. brushing her teeth.
b. sitting on the commode.
c. watching an opera.
d. riding her horse.

203

To Be or Bea or Not to Bee:

In Elizabethan England, no one worried about spelling. That's because the idea of always spelling something the same way was still very new. As a matter of fact, not even William Shakespeare (1564–1616) was consistent. The famous playwright signed his name several different ways at different times. Shagspeare, Shakespeare, and Shaxpere are just a few of them.

Pop Goes the Casket:

While on display in London, the casket of Queen Elizabeth I (1533–1603) mysteriously exploded on the night before she was to be buried. The coffin was destroyed, yet the queen's body was unharmed.

One for the Books!

Public urinals were a source of income for Emperor Vespasian (C.E. 9–79) of Rome, who had the urine collected so the ammonia could be used . . .

a. as ant killer.
b. to clean windows.
c. in fabric dyes.
d. to unclog drains.

No Joke: In 1634, Nicolas François and his wife, Claude, the Duke and Duchess of Lorraine, in France, were sentenced to death and imprisoned in the ducal palace of Nancy. On April 1, they climbed out a window and swam across the river Meurthe to safety.

Witnesses shouted an alarm, but the guards did nothing because they thought it was just an April Fool's joke.

Royal Flush: Maria Letizia Ramolino (1750–1836) is known as the "mother of monarchs." Her children were:

Napoléon, who became emperor of France; Joseph, who became king of Spain; Jérôme, who became king of Westphalia; Louis, who became king of Holland; Caroline, who became queen of Naples; Lucien, who became prince of Canino; Élisa, who became grand duchess of Tuscany; and Pauline, who became duchess of Guastalla.

Lousy Choice:

In 19th-century Sweden, a new burgomaster, or mayor, was chosen by placing a louse in the center of a table. The man whose beard the insect jumped into held the office for the next year.

One for the Books!

Emperor Akbar (1542–1605) of India forced every candidate for high office to compete with him in a game of . . .

a. night polo—using balls of fire.
b. chess—while wearing blindfolds.
c. water polo—in a pool filled with sharks.
d. croquet—using balls filled with gunpowder.

Handy Victory:

In 1015 B.C.E., Heremon O'Neill had a boating race with a rival chieftain. The first man to touch Ireland's soil would win the land. O'Neill won by cutting off his own hand and hurling it ashore, a sacrifice that made him the first king of Ulster.

By the Book:

Commentaries on the Laws of England, written by Sir William Blackstone (1723–1780), became the most influential book in the history of English law. During a session of parliament, Blackstone was proven wrong on a legal point by his own book!

Not in the Pink:

Emperor Chi'en-lung (1711–1799), considered by many to be China's wisest ruler, was switched at birth. His mother substituted the son of a court servant for her own baby girl because she was afraid to tell the emperor his child was not a boy.

Mother of Pearls: Some people believe that Mother Goose was a real person. Even though the term originated in France, one American woman is often credited with the name. Elizabeth Foster (1665–c.1756)

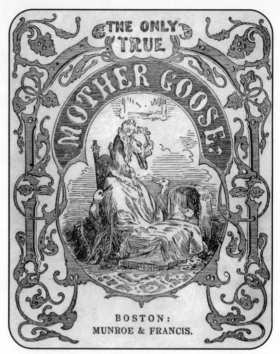

THE ONLY TRUE MOTHER GOOSE

BOSTON:
MUNROE & FRANCIS.

married Isaac Goose in 1692 and later told her grandchildren the famous rhymes—most of which came from England. The story goes that Goose's son-in-law published the rhymes in 1719, but there are no copies of the book and no proof that it was ever printed.

One for the Books!

Humpty Dumpty is really about a . . .

a. scrambled egg.
b. king who lost a war.
c. prince who fell into a moat.
d. thief who fell off a wall.

Baa, Baa Black Sheep:

Have you any wool? Yes, sir, yes, sir, three bags full. One for my master, and one for my dame. And one for the little boy who lives down the lane. Many people think this nursery rhyme was written as a complaint about taxes. The "master" was the king while "dame" stood for the rich nobility. The "little boy" was the peasant who did all the work but got just a third of the profits of his labor.

Little Jack Horner . . . *sat in a corner eating his Christmas pie. He stuck in a thumb, pulled out a plum, and said, "What a good boy am I."* To discourage robbers, deeds to King Henry VIII's properties were baked into a pie. Jack Horner was the messenger who was to deliver the deeds to the king. Legend has it that Horner wasn't so good after all, because he couldn't resist reaching into the pie and taking one of the king's deeds for himself. Seems everyone heard about the heist but King Henry!

Scents and Sensibility: In the country, people used outhouses, called privies, to relieve themselves. Privies were foul-smelling and attracted flies. Perhaps that's why so many rose, lilac, and honeysuckle bushes were planted around them. People hoped the

fragrance of the flowers would disguise the pungent odors! The expression "to pluck a rose" was a polite way of saying you were about to go to the privy.

Smelly Old Days: As late as the early 20th century, cities smelled awful. With no running water for flush toilets, poor people in the slums threw their bodily wastes and other types of garbage into the streets. It didn't take much more than a gentle breeze to carry the smells to other parts of the city.

One for the Books!

While emperor of Rome, Caligula (C.E. 12–41) made taking a bath a crime punishable by . . .

a. death.
b. imprisonment.
c. public humiliation.
d. a hefty fine.

Down and Dirty: Not only did the air smell bad in Europe during the 18th century, a lot of the people did, too. Without modern plumbing, many people didn't bathe very often. Some were so confused about hygiene that they thought bathing would cause them to catch a chill and make them sick! Instead, they covered their body odor with heavy perfumes. Pew!

Going to Pot: Victorians may have been shy about their bodies, but no one could say they lacked a sense of humor. Many Victorians used vessels called chamber pots as toilets. Some of them played tunes, others had portraits of politicians painted in the center, and still

others were painted with a large eye. Beneath the eye were the words "Use me well and keep me clean, and I'll not tell what I have seen."

Royal Stink: Not even the royals could avoid the smelly vapors that hung in the air. Once while cruising on the Thames River in England on the royal yacht, Queen Victoria fainted from the stench. Another time a section of Windsor Castle had to be closed because 53 cesspools overflowed at once.

One for the Books!

Queen Isabella of Spain (1451–1504) was proud of the fact that she . . .

a. used fragrant soaps imported from China.
b. had a solid-gold bathtub.
c. had indoor plumbing.
d. had taken only two baths in her life.

Sometimes the past is better off forgotten. And one of these four facts is *really* worth forgetting—because it isn't even true!

a. The shortest war on record was between Britain and Zanzibar. It lasted 38 minutes.

Believe It!   **Not!**

b. In the 17th century, people in England had strange cleaning methods. They used ashes, bread, and urine to clean their clothes!

Believe It!   **Not!**

c. Seventeenth-century French painter Nic Beaumont is believed to have begun the tradition of graffiti. While other artists painted lively Parisian street scenes, Beaumont was busy painting sweeping landscapes *on* the streets.

Believe It!   **Not!**

d. The state of Tennessee was once known as "Franklin."

Believe It!   **Not!**

BONUS GAME—HISTORY MYSTERY

When the United States made the Louisiana Purchase, did the government know what a good deal it got? It purchased the land from the Mississippi River to the Rocky Mountains from the French for the bargain price of $15 million. But more amazing is what this amounted to per acre. About how much do you think the United States paid for each acre of land? (Hint: It's less than $1 per acre.)

Try finding these little-known presidential facts in your history books!

Who's on First? John Hanson (1721–1783) was the first president of the United States. In 1781, Maryland signed the Articles of Confederation, and the original 13 colonies were officially united. Hanson was elected president by the assembled congress— which included George Washington (1732–1799). In fact, six more presidents were elected before Washington became the first president to serve under the Constitution, which became law in 1788.

One for the Books!

Eight U.S. presidents were born in log cabins. They were Zachary Taylor, James Polk, Franklin Pierce, Abraham Lincoln, Andrew Jackson, Millard Fillmore, James Buchanan, and . . .

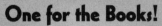

a. James Garfield.
b. Teddy Roosevelt.
c. William Taft.
d. John Quincy Adams.

Taking a Stand:

President John Adams (1735–1826) was a lawyer as well as a politician. In 1770, he was asked to defend the British soldiers accused of killing five people in the Boston Massacre. Adams was a patriot, but he decided to defend the enemy soldiers, who he felt had fired in self-defense at the threatening mob of Americans. The jury must have agreed because they acquitted seven of the soldiers and convicted two of manslaughter instead of murder. But feelings ran high in Boston and, because of his actions, Adams lost friends as well as clients.

Handy Trick:

President James Garfield (1831–1881) could write with both hands at once—using one hand to write in Latin and the other to write in Greek!

Justice for All:

President Ulysses S. Grant (1822–1885) loved to race through the streets of Washington, D.C. One day he was stopped for speeding by a police officer, who arrested him. When the officer

realized he had stopped the president, he wanted to let him go. But Grant refused to accept privileged treatment and took his punishment—a fine of $20.

One for the Books!

Abraham Lincoln (1809–1865) was the only president to receive a patent for an invention: a hydraulic system for . . .

a. removing coal from mine shafts.
b. lifting ships over shallow water.
c. raising and lowering swivel chairs.
d. elevators.

Book Smart:

Harry S. Truman (1884–1972) did not attend college, but he was highly educated. By the age of 14 he had read every book in the Independence, Missouri, library. He practiced the piano for two hours every day before he went to school, too.

Penny Pincher: Zachary Taylor (1784–1850) almost lost the nomination for president when the letter asking him to accept the honor was returned unopened by Taylor because it had been sent "postage collect" and Taylor didn't want to pay for the postage.

Cheeky Advice: Abraham Lincoln grew his beard on the advice of 11-year-old Grace Bedell (shown below at age 14) of Westfield, New York, who had definite ideas about fashion. In a letter dated October 15, 1860, she wrote: "If you will let your whiskers grow . . . you would look a great deal better for your face is so thin. All the ladies like whiskers and they would tease their husbands to vote for you and then you would be President." Lincoln took Grace's advice, and, on his way to Washington in 1861, he stopped at the Westfield train station and thanked her in person for her suggestion.

House of a Different Color: The White House wasn't always white. It was originally gray and was referred to as the Presidential Mansion. It was painted white to cover the fire damage caused by Canadians fighting for the British forces during the War of 1812. From that time on, it was known as the White House.

One for the Books!

In addition to a swimming pool and a movie theater, the White House is equipped with its own . . .

a. bowling alley.
b. Starbucks café.
c. indoor miniature golf course.
d. petting zoo.

Showing His Metal: When Andrew Jackson (1767–1845) was running for president, his opponents had a lot of "ammunition" to use against him. He'd been in at least 14 fights, duels, and free-for-alls, and had three bullets still in his body to show for it!

No Frills:

George Washington believed in getting right to the point. At just 135 words, his second inaugural speech is the shortest in history.

The Long and the Short of It:

President William Henry Harrison (1773–1841) gave the longest inaugural address—8,443 words—and served the shortest term. He made his nearly two-hour-long speech while standing outside on a cold, snowy day, and caught a severe cold that turned into pneumonia. Harrison died a mere 31 days after taking the oath of office.

Short and Sweet: Abraham Lincoln felt he had failed miserably in writing the Gettysburg Address because he thought it was too short.

Making Headlines:

A heckler threw a cabbage at William Howard Taft (1857–1930) as he was making a speech. But, without missing a beat, Taft caught the cabbage, held it up so everyone could see it, and said, "I see that one of my adversaries has lost his head."

One for the Books!

No one has ever been elected president who was . . .

a. a divorced man.
b. a bachelor.
c. an inventor.
d. an only child.

Winning Words: Unlike most politicians, Calvin Coolidge (1872–1933) was shy and didn't especially like the sound of his own voice. At a dinner party one evening, a guest made a bet that she could get him to say more than two words. "You lose," Coolidge replied.

I Do's and Don'ts: In June 1886, Grover Cleveland (1837–1908) became the only president to get married in the White House. The bride, Frances Folsom, was 21 years old—27 years younger than Cleveland. In most weddings, the wife promised to obey her husband, but Cleveland requested that this be removed from the vows.

In the Pink: On a trip to Japan, William Howard Taft's wife, Helen, so charmed the mayor of Tokyo that he sent her 3,000 cherry trees. To this day, tourists flock to Washington, D.C., to see the cherry trees bloom in the spring.

One for the Books!

Woodrow Wilson's second wife, Edith, was descended from . . .

a. Abigail Adams.
b. Clara Barton.
c. Pocahontas.
d. George Washington.

Make a Wish: Ulysses S. Grant's beloved only daughter, Nellie, was born on July 4, 1855—and for years, no one let on that the huge party complete with fireworks thrown every year on her birthday was not just for her.

Track Star: In the early 1860s, Abraham Lincoln's son Robert Todd Lincoln (1843–1926) was a student at Harvard University. While waiting to board a train at a crowded railroad station, Robert was pushed up against the train. When it started to move, he was knocked down and slipped, feet first, between the train and the edge of the platform. A quick-thinking man yanked Robert back onto the platform before he could be crushed. Who was the man? Edwin Booth, an actor and brother of John Wilkes Booth—the man who would later assassinate Robert's father!

223

Tea for Two: When Abraham Lincoln was president, he kept two goats, Nanny and Nanko. He had harnesses made for them so that they could pull his son Tad in a little cart. One day, Mrs. Lincoln was entertaining in the East Room when Tad and the goats came galloping in, upsetting the tea cart and frightening the guests. That was the end of the tea party!

All in the Family: The six children of Teddy Roosevelt (1858–1919) did not have pets—they had a zoo! With dogs, cats, snakes, horses, rabbits, ducks, horned toads, a pig, a macaw, a badger, a pony, several guinea pigs, and a rat, visitors never knew what manner of creature they might find roaming the White House!

For the Birds:
Thomas Jefferson (1743–1826) loved mockingbirds—and kept several in the White House. His favorite, Dick, loved to sing along while Jefferson played his violin. Hopping up the stairs one at a time, Dick would follow Jefferson to his bedroom, where he perched nearby and sang the president to sleep.

Got Milk? President William Howard Taft had a cow named Pauline Wayne that lived in the garage with his four automobiles. Pauline's milk was served each morning at the White House.

One for the Books!

Thomas Jefferson introduced many new foods to the U.S. that he'd discovered on his travels. Among them were macaroni, waffles, and . . .

a. cheese blintzes.
b. gyros.
c. burritos.
d. ice cream.

White House Bandit:

President Calvin Coolidge and his wife, Grace, had a pet raccoon named Rebecca. Rebecca was allowed to come inside to play—especially when there were visitors. Guests screeching at the "wild animal" in the White House never failed to make the president laugh.

Cold-blooded Gift:

After the Marquis de Lafayette (1757–1834) of France presented him with an alligator, President John Quincy Adams (1767–1848) kept it in the East Room of the White House.

One for the Books!

Franklin Roosevelt's dog, Fala, had a bald spot on his back because . . .

a. people snipped off his hair for souvenirs.
b. an infection made his hair fall out.
c. the secret service made him so nervous his hair fell out.
d. the president's grandchild learned to walk by holding on to his back.

Fala the Informer: A little black Scottie named Fala was the constant companion of Franklin Delano Roosevelt (1882–1945). During wartime, it was important to keep the president's travel plans a secret—which is why the men who guarded the president had a special name for the dog. They called him "The Informer," because a Fala-sighting meant that the president couldn't be very far away.

A Howlin' Good Time: President Lyndon B. Johnson (1908–1973) had two beagles he named Him and Her. He also had a stray mutt that he called Yuki. For laughs, he taught to Yuki to "sing" and, from time to time, he would join the dog in a howlingly good duet.

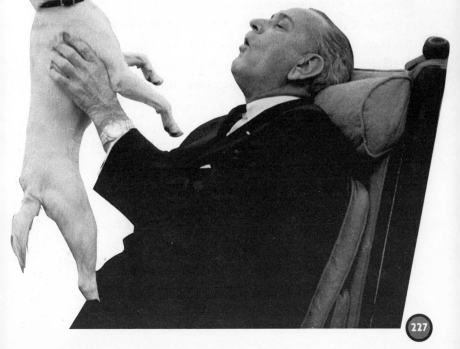

Don't Forget to Wash Your Hands! On July 2, 1881, an assassin shot President James Garfield as he walked through a Washington, D.C., train station. Garfield was taken to the White House, where Willard Bliss, the first of 16 doctors, tried to find the bullet without washing his hands or sterilizing the metal probe. Bliss didn't find the bullet and neither did the other doctors. Alexander Graham Bell looked for the bullet with an early metal detector that actually worked. But he couldn't find it either, because Garfield happened to be lying on a newly purchased mattress that had metal coils inside. On September 19, Garfield died from a heart attack probably brought on by infection. Where was the bullet? Harmlessly lodged in a muscle a few inches away from his spine. If the doctors of the time had understood the importance of sterilizing, Garfield might have made a full recovery.

Crowd Control: Immediately after President William McKinley (1843–1901) was fatally shot, he tried to keep an angry mob from attacking his assassin, saying, "Boys, don't let them hurt him!"

The Pits: On the hot July 4 of 1850, President Zachary Taylor attended groundbreaking ceremonies for the Washington Monument. He then went back to the White House, where he ate a bowl of cherries and drank a pitcher of ice-cold milk. Shortly afterward, he got severe indigestion. None of the doctors' treatments worked and, five days later, Taylor died. Rumors that he had been poisoned lasted for so long that in 1991 his body was exhumed and tested for arsenic poisoning. Nothing was found.

> # One for the Books!
>
> John Adams and his friend Thomas Jefferson both died on . . .
>
> **a.** Christmas Eve.
> **b.** their birthday.
> **c.** New Year's Day.
> **d.** the Fourth of July.

Bull Shot! Theodore Roosevelt was shot in the right lung during his 1912 campaign for the presidency. Nevertheless, he made a scheduled campaign speech a few hours later, saying, "There is a bullet in my body, but it takes more than that to kill a bull moose."

One for the Books!

Harry S. Truman's middle initial stands for . . .

a. Sherman.
b. Stephen.
c. "S."
d. Sanders.

America the beautiful. America the brave. But America the bizarre?!! Who would've guessed that three of these American facts are tried and true? Just one is totally false.

a. Sure, the words of "The Star-Spangled Banner" were written by Francis Scott Key—but it was not originally a song. It started out as a poem called "Defense of Fort McHenry."

Believe It!   **Not!**

b. Senator Strom Thurmond of South Carolina once delivered a speech to the senate that lasted 24 hours and 18 minutes.

Believe It!   **Not!**

c. The cable car, a symbol of San Francisco, California, is America's only official *moving* national historical landmark.

Believe It!   **Not!**

d. In honor of America's bicentennial in 1976, pastry chef Lynn Centrelli created the world's largest apple pie. More than 50 feet in diameter, the pie was made from more than 30,000 apples.

Believe It!   **Not!**

BONUS GAME—HISTORY MYSTERY

A number of men have all held the same job at different times throughout history. But before they took on this role, they were lawyers, teachers, governors, actors, farmers, and tailors. Eventually, they all ended up doing this same important job. What is it?

CHAPTER 4

Been There, Done That!

It's interesting to see how quickly ideas that once seemed brilliant lose their luster as the years go by.

Looking Sharp: Ancient Mayans frequently filed their teeth and used jewels to make them sparkle.

One for the Books!

In 1500 B.C.E., ancient Assyrians wore their hair . . .

a. in dreadlocks.
b. cut in the shape of tiered pyramids.
c. piled high in upsweeps.
d. in braids down to their waists.

All the Buzz: In ancient Greece, women wore live cicadas held on golden threads as ornaments for their hair.

Live Action:

The well-known game of Parcheesi was adapted from *pachisi*, a traditional game played in India since the 1500s. Most people played on cross-shaped "boards" made of cloth. But the Mogul Emperor Akbar had his own way of playing. He  stood in the center of a huge board marked out in his courtyard and directed the movements of young slave women based on the roll of his dice.

One for the Books!

Flemish women in 15th-century Belgium wore such full, billowing skirts that they had to . . .

a. sit in tall chairs while dining.
b. have their doors widened.
c. change into dressing gowns to sit at the table.
d. wear weights to keep from being swept away on windy days.

Always in Style: The ancient Egyptians were so attached to their style of dress that they didn't change it for nearly 3,000 years!

No Yolk: Incan noblemen wore solid-gold ear ornaments that were as large as eggs.

Fashion Statement:

After the Reign of Terror ended in 1794, French women honored relatives who had been beheaded by wearing a red ribbon around their necks and cropping their hair short, like that of the victims.

Rags to Riches:

In the 1400s, the Duke of Burgundy invaded what is now Switzerland. He was defeated and fled, leaving his tents and all their furnishings behind. The impoverished Swiss

soldiers tore everything apart and turned the material into patchwork uniforms slashed and puffed with different color fabrics. The costume was adopted and embellished by crack German soldiers called Landsknechte and, by the 16th century, the "slash-and-puff" style had become all the rage, worn by men and women all over Europe.

Party On!

Emperor Elagabalus (204–222) of Rome really liked to treat himself well. His daily dinner cost 300,000 sesterces—equal to $260,000 today. He also filled a pond with rose perfume and enjoyed boating on a reservoir filled with wine.

Galloping Grooms: The six-horse sleigh used by the mother of Czar Peter the Great (1672–1725) of Russia was always accompanied by 12 grooms, one for each horse plus six others to try to help the sleigh move faster. All the grooms had to run steadily for miles.

Rich Diet: During the course of her adult life, Tz'u-hsi (1835–1908), empress of China, ate ten pounds of pearls. Over a period of 47 years, $2,000,000 worth of pearls were ground up in the imperial tea. Why? Because the empress thought they would guarantee her a youthful glow.

Big Cover-up: During the Victorian era (1838–1901), modesty was so important in Europe and North America that even furniture legs had to be covered up! Words relating to personal etiquette and hygiene could not be spelled out in print. When "petticoats" appeared in an article, it would be spelled "p-tt-c-ts."

One for the Books!

For 58 years, at a total cost of $2,813,000, Rani Bhanwani (1748–1806) of Nator, India, ordered that honey be poured into every ant hole to . . .

a. attract bears to devour the ants.
b. plug up the holes.
c. provide work for the unemployed.
d. ensure that no ant would ever go hungry.

Mr. Clean: The mystic Khan Jahan Ali of Khulna, India, was one of the most fastidious men in history. In the 15th century, he built 360 artificial lakes so he could bathe in a different one each day of the Muslim year.

Good Deal!

One day, when Countess Katarzyna Kossakowska (1716–1801) of Warsaw, Poland, forgot to bring her purse to the market, she paid for a basket of oranges by removing her string of rare oriental pearls and exchanging one pearl for each orange.

Wigged Out! After losing her hair at the age of 50, Countess Natalia Saltykoff (1737–1812) of Russia kept the fact that she wore a wig secret for 25 years by imprisoning a succession of hairdressers in an iron cage in her dressing room.

Breeches of Etiquette: In the 1750s, breeches were worn so tight in Alexandria, Virginia, that men had to climb onto a raised platform to step into them.

Hair Today, Gone Tomorrow:

Emperor Theophilus, who ruled the Eastern Roman Empire from 829 to 842, went completely bald in the year 840 and promptly ordered every man, woman, and child to shave his or her head. The penalty for not shaving was death!

One for the Books!

Prince Edward (1330–1376) of England was only 16 years old when he led the defeat of the French army at Crécy. He was called the Black Prince because he . . .

a. had long, black, curly hair.
b. was always dressed in black from head to toe.
c. wore black armor.
d. had all his rooms painted black.

All Stirred Up:

In Modena, Italy, a marble statue built in 1473 was a legal yardstick for the maximum length of women's dresses. Women who wore longer dresses could be punished for stirring up dust as their hems swept the ground.

Dressed to Impress:

Queen Elizabeth I of England had 2,000 gowns, all of which were kept in a separate clothing house.

Beauty Hurts!

Though cosmetics were very big during the 16th century, safety testing was not. So when women used products containing mercury to remove brown spots, warts, and other blemishes from their skin, they had no idea that it might also remove the outer skin layer, cause their teeth to fall out, and eventually cause severe mental illness!

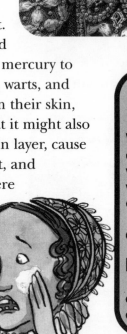

One for the Books!

Women in 16th-century England wore their wedding rings on . . .

a. a chain around their neck.
b. their middle finger.
c. their pinky.
d. their thumb.

Fashions come and go. But the most interesting ones tend to go down in history! Three of these humorous historical happenings are true. Can you guess which one is simply laughable?

a. The United States Mint considered making doughnut-shaped coins.
        Believe It!   **Not!**

b. In 1939, Ernest Wright wrote a novel called *Gadsby*. It contained more than 50,000 words—but not one of them included the letter *e*.
        Believe It!   **Not!**

c. In 1891, Silvain Dornon, a baker from Paris, walked up the 347 steps to the first platform of the Eiffel Tower—on stilts!
        Believe It!   **Not!**

d. Hoffman and Klein Industries was an American manufacturer at the turn of the 20th century. In addition to basic stationery products, the company was also the first to manufacture the whoopee cushion, in 1902.
        Believe It!   **Not!**

BONUS GAME—HISTORY MYSTERY

Throughout history, humankind has used a lot of energy. Vehicles, lights, stoves—we use energy in all kinds of ways. But in our entire history, we haven't used as much as this energy-guzzler does in just one second. What is it?

In order to trade goods and services, countries usually cooperate with each other. But every so often, a dispute that can't be settled may lead to war.

One for the Books!

In ancient Greece, soldiers lined their helmets and armor with . . .

a. mementos of loved ones.
b. sponges.
c. feathers.
d. burial instructions.

Timber! The Peace Poplar was planted in Jena, Germany, in 1815, to celebrate the end of the Napoleonic War with France. It suddenly toppled 99 years later on August 1, 1914—the start of World War I.

243

Before E-mail:

In 490 B.C.E., Persians invaded the Greek city of Marathon. Outnumbered, the Greeks sent their best runner, Philippides, to Sparta to ask for help. The Spartans refused, but the Greeks won the battle anyway. Elated, they sent Philippides, who had just

returned after running 200 miles in two days, to tell the folks back home in Athens. Eager to spread the news, Philippides made it to Athens, but had barely enough time to yell, "Nike!" (Greek for victory) before he dropped dead of exhaustion. In the photo, Robert Ripley is shown by the monument to Athenians who died in the battle.

Fine Feathered Steeds: In the

fifth century, the cavalrymen of Media, who won many battles against the Greeks, were mounted not on horses, but on ostriches.

Book Worm: Saheb Ibn Abad (C.E. 938–995), the scholarly grand vizier of Persia, always traveled with 117,000 books—even when he went to war. The library was carried on 400 camels that were trained to walk in line so that the library remained in alphabetical order and any book could be located quickly.

Heat of Battle: In 1402, the Battle of Ankara, Turkey, began by the Mongols stampeding a herd of 100 buffalo, each with a pot of liquid fire tied to its horns.

One for the Books!

In ancient times, Vikings settled disputes by binding themselves together at the waist and then . . .

a. stabbing each other.
b. seeing who could eat the most fish.
c. trying to knock each other out.
d. seeing who could sing the loudest.

Make Jokes, Not War:

The Battle of Buironfosse, in 1339, is usually thought of as one of the opening battles of the Hundred Years' War between France and England. In fact, the battle never took place. Why? Because a frightened rabbit dashed back and forth between the lines of the two opposing armies. The sight was so hilarious that the soldiers on both sides roared with laughter and withdrew without exchanging a blow.

War Games:
For 30 years, King Deva Raya (1424–1446) of Vijayanagar, India, ordered that arrows be shot toward three neighboring kingdoms each September. He then declared war on whichever country lay in the direction of the arrow that flew the farthest.

One for the Books!

Major Patrick Ferguson (1744–1780), leader of a corps of British sharpshooters, had a chance to shoot a famous American during the Revolutionary War, but he was too honorable to shoot a man in the back, and so spared the life of General . . .

a. Benedict Arnold.
b. Stonewall Jackson.
c. Israel Putnam.
d. George Washington.

Big Hold-up: In 1565, the Persian army attacked the city of Vijayanagar, India. Gulam Ali, an elephant belonging to the Persians, won the battle by winding its trunk around Rajah Ram, the enemy commander, lifting him up in the air, and holding him captive until his troops surrendered. When the elephant died years later, an elaborate tomb was erected for it in the Indian city of Ahmandnagar.

Knight in Shining . . . Skirt? King Henry VIII (1491–1547) of England often wore a coat of armor with a pleated armor skirt. The skirt looked like cloth and was equipped with hinges so the monarch could ride horseback.

Tin Soldiers:

The hat issued to United States soldiers in 1870 was topped by a tin oil lamp that helped them find their way on dark nights.

Knight Lights:

When fighting battles after dark, knights in medieval times used lighted lanterns that were attached to their saddles.

Heady Escape: General Henry Heth (1825–1899) was leading Confederate soldiers in the Battle of Gettysburg when he was hit in the head by a Union bullet. Because his hat was two sizes too large, he had stuffed newspaper inside it to make it fit better. The paper deflected the bullet, and the general, though unconscious for 30 hours, recovered and lived another 36 years.

One for the Books!

In 1942, Lieutenant I. M. Chisov, a Russian soldier, lived to tell the tale after he . . .

a. was run over by a tank.
b. was shot by a firing squad for cowardice.
c. fell 21,980 feet from his fighter plane.
d. stepped on a land mine and was thrown 500 feet by the blast.

Hat Trick: To make them look taller, Hessian soldiers (German mercenaries fighting for the British in the American Revolution) were issued hats that were 28 inches high.

Died in the Wool:

The assassination of Archduke Ferdinand of Austria was what triggered the start of World War I. But according to some historians, if the archduke had not been quite so vain, he might have survived. After Ferdinand was shot in Sarajevo on June 28, 1914, it was discovered that the buttons on his uniform were merely for show. The archduke had thought that the traditional button-down tunic was unbecoming, so he had asked the royal

tailor to create a pullover, form-fitting uniform that enhanced his profile instead. Had Ferdinand been wearing a real button-down tunic instead of one that had to be cut away, he might not have bled to death!

Psych!: Legend has it that when a brash British officer challenged General Israel Putnam (1718–1790), famed hero of the American Revolution, to a duel, Putnam insisted that first they smoke their

pipes while sitting next to a powder keg with a burning fuse. After a few moments the Englishman fled in terror, only to learn later that the keg had been emptied of powder and refilled with onions.

One for the Books!

In the winter of 1861, some Union Army soldiers in Pennsylvania could not fire their guns because . . .

a. their mittens had no trigger fingers.
b. the triggers were frozen and wouldn't work.
c. they were too cold to fight.
d. they wanted to go home for the holidays.

Never Got a Break: George Washington was the only American soldier who served throughout the entire eight and a half years of the Revolution without a single leave of absence.

Weird but True: When the Civil War broke out, the leader of the Confederate forces, General Robert E. Lee (left; 1807–1870), and his family did not own slaves. However, Julia Dent, the wife of General Ulysses S. Grant, the leader of the Union forces, owned four slaves.

Perfect Pitch: In 18th-century France, the common people were poor and had nothing to eat. Angry and desperate, they revolted against the ruling class and defeated them. Afterward, they held trials, hauling the rich before the French revolutionary tribunal. After her mother was condemned to death for being the wife of an enemy officer, Zoe de Bonchamps was ordered to sing for the tribunal's amusement. In a loud, clear voice, the little girl sang out, "Long live the King—down with the Revolution!" Her brave defiance so amused the judges that they released her mother at once.

Bird's-eye View: A Union soldier brought his pet eagle named Abe to keep him from getting too lonely during the Civil War. When the fighting started, old Abe would fly above the fray, then return to his master as soon it was over. Although the eagle did get shot, he survived his wounds and lived another fifteen years after the war. His remains are on display at the Wisconsin State Museum.

Time Out: Sometimes even soldiers need to take a break from war. One Confederate soldier wrote in his diary about the day that the sight of plump fresh blackberries prompted both sides to declare a truce. The soldiers picked the berries, shared some coffee, and traded newspapers . . . and then went back to fighting.

Hung Out to Dry: Elizabeth Van Lew was considered eccentric by many, but she was really a spy for the Union during the Civil War. On her recommendation, Mary Bowser, a slave Van Lew had freed years before, became a servant in the Confederate White House of President Jefferson Davis. Though Bowser played at being dim-witted, she was very intelligent and had a photographic memory. Perhaps if Davis had known that, he wouldn't have left military documents lying around. As it turned out, Bowser was one of the most valuable spies for the Union. She memorized military secrets she saw and overheard, then passed them back to Van Lew, who got them to General Ulysses S. Grant. Bowser also sent signals to Union soldiers in laundry code. For example, a white shirt hung beside an upside-down pair of pants meant "General Hill is moving his troops to the West."

One for the Books!

To protect them from sun and rain during the French Revolution, the National Guard of Paris was equipped with . . .

a. designer rain hats.
b. umbrella guns.
c. bulletproof raincoats.
d. portable mini-tents.

Close Shave: Captain James C. Whitley, a gunner in the Air Force during World War II, was recovering from his wounds in a hospital in Italy. One day, a barber who had been in the Italian air force was shaving him. During the conversation, Whitley discovered that the barber was a fighter pilot whose plane he had shot down in combat.

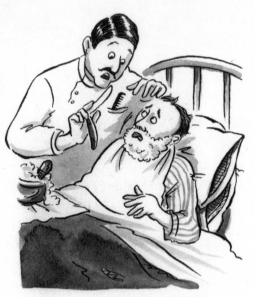

Grave Encounter: Brothers Grant and Karl Winegar, both marines stationed on Iwo Jima, Japan, had not seen each other for almost two years. Each fearing that the other might have been killed, they prowled through an American military cemetery, reading the grave markers—and suddenly met face-to-face.

One for the Books!

A sharpshooter who taught marksmanship during World War I was . . .

a. Belle Starr.
b. Mae West.
c. Annie Oakley.
d. Laura Ingalls Wilder.

Melts in Your Mouth: During World War II, soldiers needed quick-energy foods such as candy bars to keep up their strength. Other requirements were that the candy stay fresh in their backpacks and not melt in their hands. A sticky trigger finger could be a disaster! M&M's filled all these requirements and more. The fact that G.I.s bought M&M's when they came home made them an instant success with the general public.

Hail to the King: In 1360, King Edward III (1312–1377) of England was out to conquer France. But in April, just outside Paris, large hailstones rained down on his army, killing many soldiers and horses. Convinced that the hail was a sign from heaven, Edward signed the Treaty of Bretigny, giving up his claim to the French throne.

Birds of a Feather: A condor, the giant South American vulture, served as a customs agent with the Bolivian Customs Guard from 1941 to 1948 at a salary of $144 a month. The bird withdrew money every morning, flew to the meat market to buy veal for its daily meal, lived at the barracks with the rest of the company, and lined up for inspection twice a day.

One for the Books!

During World War II, money was smuggled into German prisoner of war camps in . . .

a. the linings of clothing sent by the Red Cross.
b. packets carried by homing pigeons that flew in at night.
c. packs of play money in Monopoly games.
d. rolls of gauze for bandages.

Truly man's best friend, dogs have fought right alongside their masters in times of war. And they have been celebrated for their valiant work. Three of these canine heroes really exist. Can you spot the one that's doggone false?

a. A Labrador retriever named Bailey accompanied Paul Revere on his famous midnight ride. While Revere was yelling about the British, Bailey was barking out a warning to the other dogs in the towns, causing them to howl their owners out of bed.

Believe It!   **Not!**

b. A bull terrier named Stubby spent 18 months serving in World War I. As a member of the 102nd Infantry Regiment, Stubby located wounded soldiers, protected his regiment, and even caught a spy!

Believe It!   **Not!**

c. Max, a command dog in World War II, was able to obey orders from three different armies. He was trained by the Russians, then worked for the Germans, and eventually laid telephone lines for the British.

Believe It!   **Not!**

d. The United States Armed Forces K-9 Corps has trained "parachute dogs" to act as messengers, scouts, and guards. The dogs have parachuted in to do their jobs from heights of 1,500 feet and up!

Believe It!   **Not!**

• •

BONUS GAME—HISTORY MYSTERY

A certain heroic dog breed has been using its navigational skills, search-and-rescue techniques, and ability to withstand harsh environments for hundreds of years. The breed got its name because of its assistance to a certain group of monks. Archdeacon Bernard de Menthon founded a monastery in 1050 in the Swiss Alps on the border of Italy. The monks and their canine companions helped travelers navigate the treacherous pass between the two countries for centuries. Can you figure out the name of the dog breed?

POP QUIZ

History test! Don't worry, this isn't a *real* test. This is just a chance to prove how much you know about the bizarre and unusual—everything you've read about in this book! Weird and wacky history is totally unbelievable. But you already know that, right?

1. A 9,000-year-old piece of birch resin with teeth marks in it was evidence of ancient . . .
a. dental work.
b. chewing gum.
c. fake teeth.
d. cigarette smoking.

2. Which of the following languages is *not* on the Rosetta Stone?
a. Greek
b. Demotic
c. Egyptian hieroglyphics
d. Latin

3. Which of the following was discovered buried beneath the leaning tower of Pisa?
a. A house
b. A stable
c. A tomb
d. A time capsule

4. Evidence of the first taxicab in history was unearthed in New York City.

Believe It!   **Not!**

5. Which of the following historical love stories is true?

a. Theresa Cox, daughter of an Irish merchant, wed her true love in a secret ceremony, only to discover days later that she had married into the royal Dutch family.

b. The very afternoon that Sir Daniel Malino wed his bride, Princess Jillian of York, the nobleman was awarded a medal of honor for catching a thief who had been terrorizing the British countryside.

c. Nicolas and Claude François, the Duke and Duchess of Lorraine, escaped from prison together on April Fool's Day.

d. Italian spy Antonio Fiore was taken prisoner on a secret mission to Russia. His wife, Amie, dreamed of Antonio's capture the same night, and was able to accurately describe where her husband was being held.

6. Napoléon definitely had royalty in his blood. Which one of the following was *not* one of Napoléon's siblings?

a. Jérôme, king of Westphalia

b. Christopher Alloicious, duke of Jefferson

c. Louis, king of Holland

d. Elisa, grand duchess of Tuscany

7. In 1015 B.C.E., Heremon O'Neill won the land of Ireland in a . . .

a. polo match.

b. game of cards.

c. boating race.

d. lottery.

8. Honest Abe was honestly one of the most amazing presidents of the United States. Can you spot the one fact below that's *not* true?

a. During his presidency, Lincoln invented suspenders.

b. Lincoln's son was rescued from near death by the brother of the man who would assassinate his father.

c. Lincoln kept two goats named Nanny and Nanko.

d. Lincoln grew his beard on the advice of an 11-year-old girl.

9. President James Garfield could write with both his feet at once—with one foot he'd write in German, and with the other he'd write in Japanese.

Believe It!   **Not!**

10. Which of the following White House facts is false?

a. The White House was once gray.

b. The White House was once known as the Presidential Mansion.

c. The White House has housed a raccoon, a snake, a pig, and several mockingbirds.

d. The White House was originally supposed to be built in Vermont.

11. Which of the following fashion fads never even hit the runway, so to speak?

a. Greek women once wore live cicadas in their hair.

b. In Ancient Rome, children wore bow ties until the age of ten.

c. Ancient Mayans embedded jewels in their teeth.

d. Incan noblemen wore golden ear spools as big as eggs.

12. In a vain attempt to stay young-looking, Empress Tz'u-hsi of China ate ten pounds of what jewel?
a. Emeralds
b. Diamonds
c. Pearls
d. Opals

13. Queen Elizabeth I of England had so many of these items, she had to keep them stored in a separate house. What were they?
a. Thrones
b. Gowns
c. Shoes
d. Books

14. George Washington was the only American soldier in the Revolutionary War who did not take a leave of absence during the entire eight and a half years of fighting.

Believe It!   Not!

15. Because they don't melt in your hands, this candy was enjoyed by soldiers during World War II.
a. Snickers
b. Kit Kat
c. Peppermint Patties
d. M&M's

Answer Key

Chapter 1
Can You Dig It?

Page 189: **c.** Keep out!

Page 190: **b.** flowers.

Page 192: **b.** create cartoons with speech balloons.

Page 194: **b.** a seed from which flowers were subsequently grown.

Page 197: **c.** mouse.

Page 199: **b.** mud.

Page 200: **d.** eight seconds.

Brain Buster: b. is false.

History Mystery: The United States adopted daylight saving time.

Chapter 2
The Good Old Days?

Page 203: **b.** sitting on the commode.

Page 204: **c.** in fabric dyes.

Page 206: **a.** night polo—using balls of fire.

Page 208: **b.** king who lost a war.

Page 210: **a.** death.

Page 212: **d.** had taken only two baths in her life.

Brain Buster: c. is false.

History Mystery: Approximately 3¢ per acre

Chapter 3
Back in the U.S.A.
Page 215: **a.** James Garfield.

Page 217: **b.** lifting ships over shallow water.

Page 219: **a.** bowling alley.

Page 221: **d.** an only child.

Page 222: **c.** Pocahontas.

Page 225: **d.** ice cream.

Page 226: **a.** people snipped off his hair for souvenirs.

Page 229: **d.** the Fourth of July.

Page 230: **c.** "S."

Brain Buster: d. is false.

History Mystery: President of the United States of America

Chapter 4
Been There, Done That!
Page 233: **b.** cut in the shape of tiered pyramids.

Page 234: **a.** sit in tall chairs while dining.

Page 237: **d.** ensure that no ant would ever go hungry.

Page 239: **c.** wore black armor.

Page 240: **d.** their thumb.

Brain Buster: d. is false.

History Mystery: The sun

Chapter 5

Past Imperfect

Page 243: **b.** sponges.

Page 245: **a.** stabbing each other.

Page 246: **d.** George Washington.

Page 248: **c.** fell 21,980 feet from his fighter plane.

Page 250: **a.** their mittens had no trigger fingers.

Page 253: **b.** umbrella guns.

Page 254: **c.** Annie Oakley.

Page 256: **c.** packs of play money in Monopoly games.

Brain Buster: a. is false.

History Mystery: Saint Bernard

Pop Quiz

1. **b.**
2. **d.**
3. **a.**
4. **Not!**
5. **c.**
6. **b.**
7. **c.**
8. **a.**
9. **Not!**
10. **d.**
11. **b.**
12. **c.**
13. **b.**
14. **Believe It!**
15. **d.**

What's Your Ripley's Rank?

Ripley's Scorecard

Nice work, history genius! You've dug up all kinds of fictions in these brain-busting activities. Now it's time to tally up your answers and get your Ripley's rating. Do you need to **Hit the Books**? Or maybe you already know that **The Past Is a Blast**! Add up your scores to find out!

Here's the scoring breakdown. Give yourself:
★ **10 points** for every **One for the Books!** you answered correctly;
★ **20 points** for every fiction you spotted in the **Ripley's Brain Busters**;
★ **10 points** every time you solved a **History Mystery**;
★ and **5 points** for every **Pop Quiz** question you got right.

Here's a tally sheet:
Number of **One for the Books!**
questions answered correctly: _____ x 10 = _____
Number of **Ripley's Brain Buster**
fictions spotted: _____ x 20 = _____
Number of **History Mystery**
puzzles solved: _____ x 10 = _____
Number of **Pop Quiz** questions
answered correctly: _____ x 5 = _____

Total the right column for your final score: _____

0–100
Hit the Books . . .

History is being made every day—and you don't want to miss it! The past is filled with funny, hard-to-believe stories. But maybe historical happenings just aren't your thing. No problem! There are other Ripley's books to explore. Is spooky and scary your bag? Try *Creepy Stuff*! Or *Bizarre Bugs,* if you're into the creepy crawly insect world!

101–250
Getting a Knack for Facts

The strange mysteries of history are starting to sound pretty cool, huh? You're developing a great eye for the unbelievable. And the world of Ripley's holds so many wacky and zany facts. Welcome! The bizarre is waiting around every corner.

251–400
The Past Is a Blast!

You know what fun history can be—especially when it's weird and wacky! And since history is bound to repeat itself, you're totally prepared for the future, too! To top it off, you can separate reality from the unreal in seconds—most of the time. Keep searching for the out of the ordinary. Just like Robert Ripley, you're bound to find it everywhere.

401–575
Time Traveler?

Do you have a time machine? Your knowledge of history is so good it's scary! Prehistory, the Middle Ages, modern times—nothing can stump you! Just like Robert Ripley himself, you know that there is cool stuff to be learned in every age. And you have a sharp eye for telling fact from fiction. Congratulations! You've got the makings of a fabulous historian!

Believe It!®

Photo Credits

Ripley Entertainment Inc. and the editors of this book wish to thank the following photographers, agents, and other individuals for permission to use and reprint the following photographs in this book. Any photographs included in this book that are not acknowledged below are property of the Ripley Archives. Great effort has been made to obtain permission from the owners of all materials included in this book. Any errors that may have been made are unintentional and will gladly be corrected in future printings if notice is sent to Ripley Entertainment Inc., 5728 Major Boulevard, Orlando, Florida 32819.

191 Trepanned Skulls (LC-USZC4-2536 LC-USZ62-115187); 204 Shakespeare (LC-USZ62-104495); 207 William Blackstone (LC-USZC4-2536); 210 Privy (HABS SC,10-CHAR,265B-1); 219 White House (LC-USZC4-405); 222 Grover Cleveland Wedding (LC-USZ62-5946); 226 Grace Coolidge and Raccoon (LC-USZ62-100816); 228 Garfield Assassination (LC-USZ62-7622); 230 Theodore Roosevelt (LC-USZ62-95887); 237 Tz'u-hsi (LC-USZ62-25833); 240 Queen Elizabeth I (LC-USZ62-120887); 251 Ulysses S. Grant; 251 Robert E. Lee/Library of Congress, Prints & Photographs Division

195 Rosetta Stone/© Copyright The British Museum

197 Golden Mummy/© Sandro Vannini/CORBIS

198 Hal Saflieni Hypogeum/© Paul Almasy/CORBIS

200 Bust of Diocletian; 208 Mother Goose; 249 Archduke Ferdinand and Wife/© Bettman/ CORBIS

215 John Hanson/Cedric B. Egeli, c. 1974, oil on canvas. Courtesy Maryland Commission on Artistic Property, MSA SC 1545-1033

216 Courtroom; 220 Washington's Inauguration; 235 Landsknechte costume; 238 18th-century Breeches; 252 Eagle/Dover Publications

218 Grace Bedell/Copyright Unknown

223 Nellie Grant/Courtesy of Dr. James Brust, San Pedro, CA

227 Lyndon B. Johnson and Yuki/Yoichi R. Okamoto/LBJ Photo Library

255 M&M's/™/®M&M'S is a registered trademark of Mars, Incorporated and its affiliates (Mars, Incorporated 2002). Mars, Incorporated is not associated with Nancy Hall, Inc., Ripley's Believe It or Not!, or the authors. Images of Packaging printed with permission of Mars, Incorporated.

World's Weirdest Gadgets

Contents

Introduction

The Man Who Reinvented Himself

Robert Ripley was one of the most unconventional personalities of the 20th century. He traveled the globe visiting amazing places, meeting incredible people, and gathering bizarre stories and artifacts to use in his Believe It or Not! cartoons. Although Ripley's subjects varied widely, they all had one underlying theme: The world is an unbelievably amazing place.

A self-taught artist, Ripley began his career earning $18 a week as a sports cartoonist. One day, when he couldn't think of a subject for the next day's cartoon, he put together a group of assorted athletic facts and feats from his personal files. Then he handed in his work and hoped for the best.

"The best" was far more spectacular than he could have imagined. This first Believe It or Not! cartoon was an overnight sensation. After Ripley expanded his column to include subjects from all areas of life, he became the first millionaire cartoonist in history. He wrote Believe It or Not! books, opened museums, starred

in a radio show, and soon after television was invented, had his own TV show.

Ripley's favorite subjects were those that celebrated the uniqueness of the human spirit. He particularly admired the kind of creativity and persistence it takes to become an inventor. He was fascinated by people who found completely fresh ways to view the occurrences of daily life—people like Sir Isaac Newton, who, after being hit on the head by an apple, figured out the principle of gravity. Or Archimedes, the Ancient Greek philosopher who noticed that when he lowered himself into the tub, the water level rose, prompting him to come up with a method to measure the volume of objects by seeing how much water they displaced.

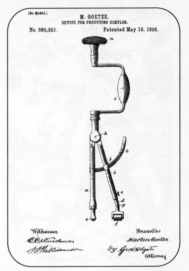

Robert Ripley also took great pleasure in showcasing funny inventions like dimple-makers, dogmobiles, and alarm clocks that sprayed water in a sleeper's face. Marvels of ingenuity like the mustache protector might have been forgotten if Ripley had not recorded them in his cartoons. And Ripley was especially impressed by the creations of inventors under 12 years old.

So get ready! You're about to discover a world of incredible inventions created by people just like you. Who knows? Maybe you'll be inspired to invent something totally incredible.

Believe It!®

CHAPTER 1 Accidentally Awesome

Occasionally, things turn out even better than we expect.

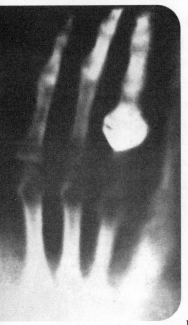

A Bright Idea: In 1895, German scientist Wilhelm Roentgen turned on his cathode-ray machine. A sheet of paper coated with a barium chemical compound immediately started to glow. Imagine Roentgen's surprise when he put his hand between the apparatus and the paper— and saw the outline of his bones. He later took the first X-ray photograph of his wife's left hand. In 1901, Roentgen was awarded the first Nobel Prize in physics for his discovery.

Imagine That!

In ancient China, the penalty for revealing the secret of making silk to foreigners was . . .

a. going naked.
b. death.
c. eating silkworms.
d. cutting out the tongue.

A Sticky Problem: While Spence Silver, a scientist at 3M Laboratories, was trying to come up with a superstrong glue in 1968, he came up with an adhesive that stuck, but only sort of. For years, Silver showed it to coworkers, hoping someone would figure out what to do with it. At last, Arthur Fry in new-

product development thought of Silver's glue when his paper bookmarks kept falling out of his hymnal at choir practice. After Fry coated the bookmarks with the glue, they not only stayed in place, but could be removed without damaging the pages. The resulting product, Post-it Notes, is now among 3M's best-selling products.

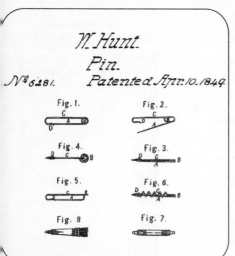

Wired: In 1849, Walter Hunt, an inventor who lived in New York City, was idly twisting a wire while trying to think of a way to earn enough money to pay off a $15 debt. The result was the safety pin. Hunt patented his invention, but had no idea of its potential value. He sold the rights for just $400.

Potluck: In the 1890s, Conrad Hubert bought the patent rights to a novelty item called the electric flowerpot. Out of the flowerpot "grew" a stem, which was actually a narrow tube containing a battery. A bulb lit up an artificial plant at its top. Unfortunately, there weren't many buyers. So Hubert decided to separate the tube and the lightbulb from the flowerpot and patent his new product as the Portable Electric Light. This early flashlight was an instant success, and Hubert formed the American Ever-Ready Company and made his fortune.

Imagine That!

According to the U.S. Patent and Trademark Office, an invention is sometimes the product of . . .

a. absolute genius.
b. sheer stupidity.
c. smoke and mirrors.
d. pure luck.

Explosive Discovery:
In 1826, an English pharmacist named John Walker was trying to invent a new explosive. After stirring up a batch of chemicals, he set the mixture aside. Later, he saw that a glob had hardened at the end of his stirring stick, and he tried to get it off by scraping the stick against the floor. Much to his surprise, the glob burst into flames. Walker had accidentally invented the first friction match.

All Fired Up: When untreated, rubber, which is made from tree sap, melts in hot weather and cracks in the cold. During the winter of 1839, British scientist Charles Goodyear was experimenting with ways to make it better. While heating rubber mixed with sulfur, he and his brother began to argue. As Goodyear gestured wildly with his stirrer, he dropped some of the goop onto the hot stove. Later, he scraped the rubber off and was amazed to find that it was dry and flexible. He put some outside, and in the morning, found that the rubber had not cracked in the cold. Goodyear's process is called *vulcanization*.

Imagine That!

Microwaves produce heat by . . .

a. causing molecules in food to rub against each other.
b. creating tiny waves of gas.
c. producing electromagnetic fields.
d. creating thermodynamic fumes.

Marvelous Meltdown: The magnetron tube, which produces microwave radiation, was first used in radar sets during World War II. In 1946, while testing one of the tubes at Raytheon Laboratories, a scientist named Percy Spencer reached into his pocket for a candy bar and found a warm, gooey mess. Aware that microwaves produced heat, Spencer wondered if the melting was caused by the magnetron. To test his theory, he put a bag of popcorn kernels next to the magnetron. Before he knew it, the kernels were popping all over the floor. Spencer had his answer—and the key to microwave cooking!

Shoe-In: Patsy Sherman, a researcher at 3M Laboratories, was working with fluorochemicals to be used in the airplane industry. In 1953, a lab assistant spilled a bit of an experimental mixture onto her new sneakers. The assistant tried to clean it off, but neither soap nor solvents worked. As time went on, the area inside the chemical spill stayed white, while the rest of the shoe got dirty. Sherman took notice and along with Sam Smith, another 3M chemist, set out to improve the new fabric protector. The product, launched in 1956, was spectacularly successful. Its name? Scotchgard.

Dry Idea: One day, Jean-Baptiste Jolly, a French tailor, knocked over an oil lamp and spilled turpentine on a tablecloth. As he tried to clean up the mess, he noticed that the more he rubbed, the brighter the fabric became. Jolly recognized the value of his discovery at once. He called his new cleaning method *dry cleaning*, and in 1825 opened the world's first dry-cleaning store in Paris.

Child's Play: While working at his father's company in Ohio, Joe McVicker came up with a new cleaning product, but it was so weird and pasty he wasn't sure what to do with it. On a hunch, he wiped it over some smudges on the wallpaper in his office, and they disappeared. But even though his Magic Wallpaper Cleaner worked well, it didn't sell. After McVicker's sister-in-law told him that the children at her nursery school found clay hard to work with because their hands were so small, he sent samples of his nontoxic cleaner for the kids to play with. This time his hunch paid off. The kids had a ball with it. By 1957, color and fragrance had been added, and the name of the former wallpaper cleaner was changed to one we all know: Play-Doh.

> ## Imagine That!
>
> The fragrance that was added to Play-Doh is . . .
>
> **a.** cinnamon.
> **b.** mint.
> **c.** ginger.
> **d.** vanilla.

Good Vibrations: In 1945, engineer Richard James was trying to produce a spring that would keep the needles on ship gauges from bouncing around with the motion of the waves. One day, he accidentally knocked his model off a shelf. The spring moved coil by coil from the shelf to a table to a chair, only to land upright on the floor. Next, he tried it on the stairs. When his wife saw it, she instantly realized what a wonderful toy it would make. She named it Slinky and started the company that has continued producing the creation to this very day.

Presidential Bearing: In 1902, the *Washington Star* published a cartoon featuring President Theodore "Teddy" Roosevelt, rifle in hand, walking away from a frightened bear cub. It was based on a real-life incident. During a hunting trip, Roosevelt's hosts wanted to ensure he got a trophy, so they trapped a cub for him to shoot. Roosevelt refused. Morris Michtom displayed the cartoon clipping in his shop window next to a stuffed bear cub made by his wife. To his surprise, everyone wanted to buy "Teddy's Bear." To meet the demand, Michtom started his own manufacturing company, later known as the Ideal Toy Corporation.

Not So Silly: What stretches, bounces, shatters when hit with a hammer, and picks up lint from clothing, and print from newspapers and comic books? In 1943, General Electric engineer James Wright was trying to create an inexpensive rubber substitute. In one experiment, Wright added boric acid to silicon oil. What he got was a slippery substance that bounced. What could you do with it? Nothing practical, Wright thought. Maybe not, but in 1950, Peter Hodgson bought $147 worth of the gooey stuff, put it inside plastic eggs, and sold it as a toy called Silly Putty. Since then, more than three hundred million of the toy have been sold.

Imagine That!

Which of the following statements is not true about Silly Putty?

a. Athletes use it to strengthen hand muscles.
b. Zookeepers have used it to create paw imprints of gorillas.
c. Orthodontists use it to create dental molds.
d. Astronauts used it to anchor objects on Apollo 8.

Chipped Off: George Crum was the chef at an elegant restaurant in Saratoga Springs, New York. One day in 1853, a very demanding customer kept sending back his French fries because they weren't thin enough. The third time they came back, Crum sliced the potatoes paper-thin, then purposely fried them to a crisp. Much to Crum's surprise, the customer was delighted, and so was everyone else who sampled them. Word of the taste sensation spread throughout the area, and people traveled great distances to sample the new Saratoga Chips. After the automatic potato slicer was invented in the 1920s, potato chips became America's best-selling snack food.

Imagine That!

To make enough potato chips each year to satisfy the craving of United States consumers, you would need more than . . .

a. 100,000 pounds of potatoes.
b. three billion pounds of potatoes.
c. 500,000 tons of potatoes.
d. 10 million bushels of potatoes.

Cold Comfort: In 1875, a law was passed in Evanston, Illinois, banning the sale of ice-cream sodas on Sunday. Carbonated beverages were thought to be related to alcoholic beverages and, as such, could not be sold on a day of worship. Undaunted, shop owners simply removed the soda

and served the scoops of ice cream with syrup. They called the new treats *sundaes* to distinguish them from the spelling of the Christian Sabbath day.

Play with Your Food: The sandwich was named after the Earl of Sandwich, who loved to gamble. He invented it so he could eat a meal without interrupting his card game.

Dye-ing of Thirst: Pete Conklin invented pink lemonade in the 1800s when he unwittingly made lemonade from a bucket of water in which a circus performer had soaked his red tights.

Hole-in-One: One night in the 1800s, a storm came up while Captain Hanson Gregory was at sea. He anchored the fried cake he'd been eating on one of the spokes of the helm so that he could use both hands to steer. When he retrieved his cake, Gregory was pleased to note that the part he liked least—the soggy middle—was gone. From then on, he had the cook fry his cakes with a hole in the center. A less exciting story has Gregory's mother complaining that the centers of her cakes didn't cook through, and the young Gregory suggesting that she try making them with a hole in the middle. In either event, Gregory gets the credit for inventing the doughnut as we know it.

Imagine That!

Which popular candy got its shape by accident when the machine that made it malfunctioned?

a. M&M's
b. Tootsie Rolls
c. PEZ
d. Life Savers

Half-Baked: In 1930, Ruth Wakefield, owner and proprietor of the Toll House Inn in Massachusetts, was baking chocolate cookies when she realized that she was out of baker's chocolate. So she broke up some of the semisweet chocolate she had on hand and stirred the pieces into the dough. When she removed the cookies from the oven, Wakefield saw that the chocolate had not dissolved. She served the chocolate chip cookies anyway and was amazed at the delighted response of her customers. Chocolate chip cookies have since become an American favorite.

Fill 'er Up: Italo Marchiony of New York was granted a patent for an ice-cream cone in 1903. But several others claim it was invented at the 1904 World's Fair in St. Louis, Missouri. In one story, Ernest Hamwi was selling wafflelike pastries next to an ice-cream vendor who ran out of dishes. Hamwi rolled a pastry into a cone shape, and the ice-cream vendor filled it with a scoop of ice cream. They called it the World's Fair Cornucopia.

Windfall: In 2737 B.C.E., Chinese emperor Shen Nong was outside boiling water when falling leaves accidentally landed in his kettle. As the leaves began to brew, the aroma was so enticing that the emperor took a taste. The flavor was both soothing and refreshing—and people have been drinking tea ever since.

Imagine That!

The first U.S. patent authorized by President George Washington protected a new method for making . . .

a. candles.
b. soap.
c. stirrups.
d. oil lamps.

Your turn! Bust your brain on these "inventive" activities. Some creations made history—others are just made up. Can you tell the difference?

Robert Ripley dedicated his life to seeking out the bizarre and unusual. But every unbelievable thing he recorded was true. In the Brain Busters at the end of each chapter, you'll play Ripley's role—trying to verify the fantastic facts presented. Each Ripley's Brain Buster contains a group of four shocking statements. But of these so-called "facts," **one** is **fiction**. Will you **Believe It!** or **Not!**?

Wait—there's more! Following the Brain Busters are special bonus games where you can try to keep those Ripley's facts straight by playing matchup. To see how you did, flip to the end of the book for answer keys and a scorecard.

How *did* you think of that?!! Well, people come up with inventions in all sorts of ways. Here are four wacky innovation stories. Can you tell which three are true and which one is pure invention?

a. The Frisbee was modeled after pie tins that students at Yale University would throw around for fun in the 1870s. The tins came from a local pie maker named (what else?) William Frisbie.

      Believe It!   **Not!**

b. Amanda Jones is the woman responsible for the vacuum method of canning that revolutionized the food industry. But Jones claimed that the idea was not hers at all—she insisted that her dead brother came to her in a vision and told her to try it.

Believe It!   **Not!**

c. Early versions of the Hula Hoop were made out of vines and wood quite some time ago. Records of their existence date back to ancient Egypt and Greece.

Believe It!   **Not!**

d. Steven R. Goodman, inventor of the sidewalk, claims the idea came to him after he sat on his head for five hours straight, staring at a freshly paved road.

Believe It!   **Not!**

• •

BONUS GAME

Name Game! **Many inventions improved upon items that already existed. And most have changed names over the course of time. The following are five common items. Can you match them up to the names they once had?**

1. Kool-Aid
2. Life Savers
3. Bubble gum
4. Vacuum cleaner
5. Zipper

a. Blibber-Blubber
b. Pneumatic carpet renovator
c. Fruit Smack
d. Pep-O-Mint
e. Clasp-locker

It's not too hard to figure out why some inventions do *not* stand the test of time.

Fish in a Barrel: In the 1800s, Jules Le Batteux of France believed that hands-on experience was the best kind. Perhaps that's why he invented a new way to fish. Lowering himself into the water in a barrel fitted with a leather sleeve and glove, Batteux put his hand into the glove and grabbed the fish as they swam by.

Imagine That!

An alarm clock invented in 1500 sounded the hour and also . . .

a. ran a bath.
b. let out the dog.
c. watered the plants.
d. lit a candle.

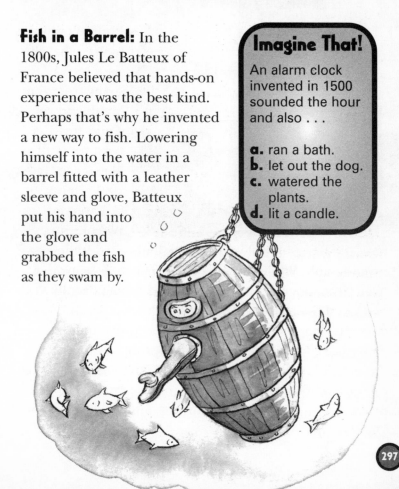

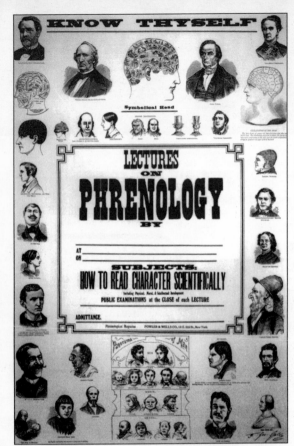

Getting Your Head Examined:

Phrenology is the study of personality and character traits based on the shape of a person's skull. Phrenologists figured that the skull took its shape from the brain, and you could "read" a person's skull like a map. In 1901, Henry C. Lavery of Wisconsin built the first phrenology machine and called it the psychograph. While the subject sat in a chair beneath a headpiece, the machine measured 32 mental faculties and rated them from "deficient" to "very superior." The data was sent to a printer that produced readings on paper tape. Once considered a foolproof way to make important life decisions—such as whom to marry or what career to choose—today, psychographs are found only in places like the Ripley's Odditoriums and the Museum of Questionable Medical Devices.

Diet Fork: If you tend to gulp your food, a fork with a built-in timer might be the perfect thing for you. This fork tells its owner when it's okay to take another bite. By the time you're halfway through, the odds are your food will be so cold you won't even want it anymore.

Grapefruit Guard: You won't get a spray in the eye from your grapefruit if you wear a grapefruit mask at breakfast.

Imagine That!

At the age of 82, Edgar Sims of Sun City, Arizona, invented a hearing aid in the shape of . . .

a. mouse ears.
b. a conch shell.
c. a megaphone.
d. antennae.

Bottoms Up: For those beginning skiers who spend a lot of time on their butts, the Laid-Back Skiers Association invented special skis to be worn—where else?—on the rear end!

Dull Idea: Herbert Greene of Pennsylvania invented a knife with a slot in the blade that would keep those pesky peas from rolling off your knife while eating.

Crying Time:
Patented in 1971, an electrical device designed to put a baby to sleep with a series of regular pats on the bottom seemed to make the baby cry even harder.

Whiff-le Ball:

A golf ball that glows and gives off a scent so it can be easily found was invented and patented in 1990.

Sleeping Beauties:

Why bury the dead when you can keep your loved one preserved and hermetically sealed in a decorative block of glass? This invention, which received U.S. patent #748,284 in 1903, would also make a nifty coffee table.

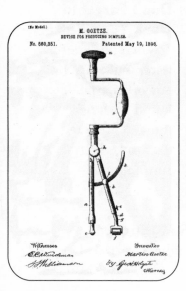

(No Model.)

M. GOETZE.
DEVICE FOR PRODUCING DIMPLES.

No. 560,351.   Patented May 19, 1896.

Witnesses
C.C. Wickman
S. Williamson

Inventor
Martin Goetze
by Geo. Holgate
Attorney

Smile!

A device for making dimples was invented by Martin Goetze in 1896.

Imagine That!

Over 300 patents have been registered with the U.S. Patent Office for devices to stop . . .

a. fingernail-biting.
b. snoring.
c. bed-wetting.
d. stuttering.

Stiff Upper Lip: In 1872, Eli J. F. Randolph of New York invented a mustache protector. A hard rubber device with prongs that fit into the nostrils, it was designed to keep mustaches neat and tidy while eating and drinking. To date, it has not found its market.

Don't Forget to Dunk Your Watch: A watch powered by water, milk, tea, or any other type of liquid must be dunked every few days to keep it running on time.

Following Suits: Invented by Mark Woehrer of Nebraska, Tag-a-long, the robotic suitcase carrier that follows its owner wherever he or she goes, has yet to catch on.

What a Scream! For all those stressed-out souls who need a harmless outlet, the scream muffler is just what the doctor ordered. All they have to do is scream at the top of their lungs into the scream muffler. No one will hear them because it is packed with special acoustical foam that will turn even the loudest screech into the softest whimper.

Edison's Follies: Thomas A. Edison was granted 1,093 U.S. patents. Many of his revolutionary inventions

changed our lives forever, but not all of them were winners. Take, for instance, his concrete houses, which were supposed to be cheap and easy to build. Unfortunately, before even one house could go up, a builder had to buy almost $200,000 worth of equipment—and the iron forms required to hold the poured concrete weighed nearly half a million pounds!

Guess What Time It Is: The one-hand clock invented by Benjamin Franklin in 1770 gave you a choice. For example, the time could be 3:35, 7:35, or 11:35. Franklin figured that everyone knew what hour of the day it was. A 1919 version (at right) took away the guessing by setting up the hours as on a normal clock, but showing all 60 minutes for each hour.

Kitchen Helper: A device that served as a combination grater, slicer, mouse trap, and fly trap was given U.S. patent #586,025 in 1897.

Plow and Shoot: In 1862, a patent on an invention that worked as a combined plow and gun was filed at the U.S. Patent Office.

Tip-Off:

Just the thing for a cold winter stroll, U.S. patent #556,248 is for an invention that makes it possible for a gentleman to tip his hat while keeping his hands in his pockets.

How Convenient!

A topcoat patented in 1953 by Howard Ross of Gainesville, Virginia, could be worn by one person or expanded to fit two.

Imagine That!

A patent was filed at the U.S. Patent Office for a bicycle security device. If it wasn't disarmed by its owner, it would send up through the bicycle seat . . .

a. a needle.
b. superglue.
c. an electric shock.
d. an icy spray of water.

Suited to Your Mood: Because it is thermally sensitive, a bathing suit invented by Donald Spector of Union City, New Jersey, changes color as its wearer's body temperature fluctuates according to his or her mood.

Over the Top: In 1895, Henry Latimer Simmons of Wickes, Montana, patented a railroad system featuring cars that had tracks on their sloped roofs. This made it possible for one train to leapfrog over another while traveling on a single track.

Spare the Child: A spanking paddle, patented in the U.S. in 1953, had a jointed handle designed to break if the child was spanked too firmly.

Wet Blanket: In 1907, an alarm clock that sprayed water on a sleeping person received U.S. patent #889,928.

Imagine That!

Rick Tweddell of Ohio invented plastic molds that change the shape of growing vegetables to make them look like . . .

a. dogs and cats.
b. famous people.
c. letters of the alphabet.

Pucker Up:

In the 1930s, Hollywood makeup artist Max Factor invented a hand-operated kissing machine with molded rubber lips that could be pressed together to test lipstick.

Double Play:

James Bennett invented a double baseball glove in 1905. The player wore one part in each hand and caught the ball by clapping his or her hands together.

Rude Awakening: Have trouble rising and shining? Perhaps you need a contraption invented by Ludwig Ederer of Omaha, Nebraska, to automatically throw you out of bed. Connected to steam pipes, the bed would lower and dump the sleeper when the pressure fell.

Dying to Escape:

Being buried alive was of grave concern to those living in the late 1800s and early 1900s. Luckily for them, Count Karnice-Karnicki of Russia invented a solution in 1896. A glass ball was connected by a spring to a box above the grave. If the chest of the buried person moved, the spring was released and the box lid popped open, letting light and air reach the coffin. It also rang a bell and raised a flag to alert unsuspecting mourners.

Imagine That!

Researcher Aikis Togias developed a nose spray made out of . . .

a. mold spores.
b. roasted garlic.
c. orange oil.
d. jalapeño peppers.

Heads Up: In 1962, George R. Masters invented a device for a player to practice passing a football to him- or herself. It consisted of a headband with a football attached by an elastic cord.

But Why? Thomas Urquhart, a 17th-century English translator, invented a language that consisted entirely of palindromes—words that can be read forward or backward.

Safety Briefs: In 1998, Katsuo Katugoru of Tokyo, Japan, whose greatest fear is drowning, designed underpants that would inflate 30 times their original size if there were a tidal wave. Unfortunately, Katugoru accidentally set them off while riding on a crowded subway at rush hour. Fortunately, one passenger had the presence of mind to deflate the underpants by stabbing them with a pencil.

Eyesore: Invented in 1931, the eyeball massager was operated by squeezing its two rubber centers.

Putting a Lid on It: Inventor of the alternating current motor and many other successful inventions, Nikola Tesla tried but was unsuccessful in perfecting a device that could photograph thoughts on the eyeball.

Fish Story: For better night fishing, Canadian Paul Giannaris invented a chemical formula that makes worms glow in the dark.

Scaredy-Cat: Uninvited creatures are supposed to scurry from your garden when they see the amazing mechanical leaping cat, which is guaranteed to keep your garden pest-free.

Imagine That!

The Ohio Department of Transportation is studying ways to use fermented cheese as a . . .

a. warning flare.
b. paving material.
c. dye for highway stripes.
d. deicer on highways.

Kooky contraptions! Though the following discoveries may have missed the history books, three of the stories are true. One, however, is nothing but a tall tale.

a. With his head in the sky, William Calderwood of Sun City, Arizona, dreamed of floating furniture. He crafted it so that it could stay in the air for up to six weeks.

Believe It!   **Not!**

b. Singing and stitching must have been in fashion when, in the 1800s, a sewing machine was invented that also played music.

Believe It!   **Not!**

c. In 1974, a picture frame equipped with voice recording technology was invented in Hobart, Indiana, by D. Butler. The device allowed people to gaze at photographs while listening to a recorded message up to two and one-half minutes in length.

Believe It!   **Not!**

d. In 1887, Charles Wulff patented a bird-powered balloon propelled by eagles, vultures, and condors.

Believe It!   **Not!**

BONUS GAME

Who needs it? Some inventions seem utterly useless, while others make us wonder how we ever lived without them. But in fact there was a time before our everyday items existed. Can you place these familiar objects in the order in which they made their much-needed debuts?

1. Envelopes
2. Postcards
3. Jigsaw puzzles
4. Common cross-blade scissors
5. Basketball hoops

a. 3 (1839)
b. 4 (1869)
c. 1 (1500)
d. 5 (1906)
e. 2 (1760)

CHAPTER 3 Way to Go!

There's no limit to the lengths, heights, and depths people will go to when looking for new ways to get around.

Having It Your Way:

AUTOnomy, General Motors' new concept car, is controlled by wires and software, and powered by hydrogen fuel cells, which won't give off harmful emissions such as carbon dioxide. And for the style-conscious, the car would be manufactured in two parts—the chassis, called a "skateboard," and the body—so you could buy a short, medium, or long chassis to match whichever style body you prefer.

Imagine That!

In 1900, Uriah Smith of Battle Creek, Michigan, designed a horseless carriage that, in order not to frighten horses, featured . . .

a. simulated hoofbeats.
b. no bright colors or shiny metal.
c. a model of a horse's head in front.
d. a whisper-quiet motor.

Lunar Buggy:
Using nothing more high-tech than scrap aluminum, an old umbrella, bicycle handlebars, automobile hubcaps, a starter motor, batteries, and army surplus stock,

Eduardo Carrion San Juan of San Jose, California, designed and invented the prototype of the lunar roving vehicle used to explore the moon.

Front-Wheel Drive: A dogmobile, patented in the United States in 1870, was propelled by two dogs running in a cage inside the front wheels.

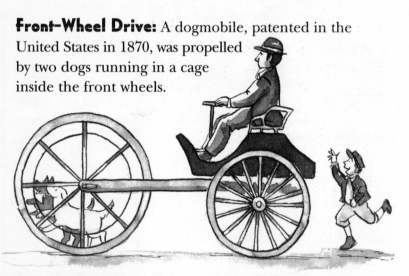

Details, Details: A flying automobile was successfully flown in the United States in 1947, but crashed because the pilot had forgotten to fill the gas tank.

Slow and Steady:

Invented by David Bushnell of Saybrook, Connecticut, the *Turtle* was the first submarine ever to be used in a war. About seven feet high and seven feet long, the wooden vessel was bound by iron hoops and hand-powered by one person. On September 7, 1776, Ezra Lee set off in the *Turtle* to plant a bomb on a British ship in New York harbor. After failing to attach the device to the ship's hull, Lee released it in the harbor, where it blew up, reportedly startling the British fleet, which promptly sailed to safer waters.

Imagine That!

Hinrich L. Bohn, a soil scientist at the University of Arizona, used dirt-filled car bumpers to help . . .

a. absorb impact.
b. grow flowers.
c. filter car fumes.
d. increase traction.

Look Out, Bell-ow!

A diving bell, enabling divers to work at the bottom of the sea for hours, was invented in 1720 by English astronomer Edmund Halley, who also predicted the cycle of the comet that became known as Halley's Comet.

Making a Splash:

A diving suit invented by Hardsuits International is an atmospheric diving system that stabilizes air pressure around the body so that divers can work comfortably at depths of 2,000 feet. The suit is powered by twin motors on either side of the oxygen tank, and divers can steer in any direction by using the built-in foot pedals. Because the suit weighs 1,100 pounds, divers have to be lowered into the water in a metal cage. Intending to use them for salvage and rescue missions, the U.S. Navy purchased four suits in 2001—at a cost of 2.7 million dollars each.

Imagine That!

A device for lifting vessels over sandbars was patented on May 22, 1849, by . . .

a. Robert Fulton.
b. Thomas A. Edison.
c. Benjamin Franklin.
d. Abraham Lincoln.

Making Waves:

Flat surf? No problem. The PowerSki Jetboard, invented by former surfer Bob Montgomery, makes its own waves. Combining the ease of waterskiing with the freedom of surfing, the Jetboard has a small but powerful engine that weighs just under 40 pounds. As of June 2002, you could get one for just under six thousand dollars.

Sub Cycle:

In 1896, Alvary Templo of New York built the first underwater bicycle. A submarine-shaped air tank piped air to Templo's helmet, enabling him to stay down for as long as six hours.

Flying Solo: Imagine a flying machine that is almost as compact and easy to operate as a bicycle. Impossible? Not if Michael Moshier, founder of Millennium Jet in California, has his way. His SoloTrek XFV (short for Exoskeletor Flying Vehicle) supports two gas engine-powered fans that extend above the frame like giant ears. The pilot stands on a pair of footrests, tightens the body belt, and grabs onto the joysticks that control the vehicle. To date, the SoloTrek has only flown about eight inches off the ground for about nine seconds. But with support from the Pentagon and NASA, chances are that one day Moshier's dream machine will soar 8,000 feet above the trees at 80 miles per hour, just as it was designed to do.

Sky-Driving: California-based Paul Moller is perfecting his two-passenger M400 Skycar, which will fly like an airplane but can take off vertically like a helicopter.

Fire-Breather: Used by the Chinese in 11th-century warfare, the Fire Dragon was the world's first steam-driven land vehicle and also the world's first two-stage rocket. On its way to the target, the rocket ignited arrows that flew from the Dragon's mouth.

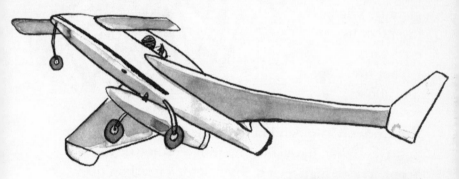

Rockets for Rookies:

Jeff Greason of Mojave, California, has invented the first reusable rocket engine. Greason's EZ-Rocket (above) is powered by twin 400-pound thrust rocket engines that burn isopropyl alcohol and liquid oxygen. The invention is capable of rising 65 miles into the air—high enough for a spectacular view, but not high enough to go into orbit. Greason estimates that someday such a tour could cost just $900 per flight, a real bargain when it comes to space travel.

Imagine That!

Before entering the automobile industry, David Buick invented the . . .

a. pushpin.
b. pacemaker.
c. porcelainized bathtub.
d. pulley.

Treading Water:

In July 1883, it took Jack Ferry eight hours to cross the English Channel on the giant tricycle he invented. Its extra-large rubber tires kept him afloat.

Roll Model:

Two San Francisco designers, Johan Liden and Yves Behar, have come up with a prototype for Scoot, a sleek high-tech scooter. Made of carbon fiber and aluminum, Scoot combines a wide, scooped-out footrest with tough oversized wheels. It folds in two and its wheels tuck neatly away so that it can be slung over the shoulder when not in use. Powered by hydrogen, Scoot is made for speed, and once it becomes widely available, it's sure to leave its competitors far behind.

Imagine That!

In the late 1800s, an advertisement for the first bicycles described them as . . .

a. a well-balanced vehicle for a well-balanced traveler.
b. an ever-saddled horse that eats nothing.
c. a two-wheeled horseless cart.
d. a peddler's delight.

Miles to Go: Created by Italian bike-maker Aprilia, the first electric bike powered by pollution-free hydrogen gas is scheduled to be available in 2003. It weighs less than regular electric bikes and travels twice the distance—43 miles—before it needs more fuel.

Wheels of Fortune: Dean Kamen believes his gyroscope-stabilized, battery-powered scooter known as the Segway will replace the car in cities. A single battery charge will take Segway owners 15 miles over level ground. Speed and direction are controlled by the driver shifting his or her weight. Currently, the Segway is being tested by mail carriers in New Hampshire.

Plugged In: Steve Roberts of Washington traveled 17,000 miles on a high-tech, 580-pound bicycle called the BEHEMOTH. It featured 105 gears, five computers, satellite connection to the Internet, an amateur radio, and a handlebar keyboard that let him write while riding. Where was the computer display? In his helmet!

Roll Playing: Jean-Yves Blondeau has invented a new way to skate. In addition to standard in-line skates, he wears a bodysuit made of hard latex with wheels attached at the knees, back, elbows, hands, and chest—27 in total. As he zips through the streets of Paris at speeds of up to 30 miles per hour, he can morph into 20 perfectly balanced positions. To excel at Blondeau's new sport, you need the agility of a hockey player and the balance and flexibility of a gymnast.

Big Wheels: An eight-man tricycle built in New England in 1896 weighed 2,500 pounds, was 17 feet long, and had rear wheels that were 11 feet in diameter.

Imagine That!

A trolley car designed in the 1870s had an engine that ran on . . .

a. ammonia.
b. hay.
c. hydrogen.
d. apple peelings.

Moving right along . . . some inventions have taken us quite far. But one of the following four is *far* from true!

a. In an effort to liven up the slopes, Daniel Cook of Princeton, New Jersey, invented snow skis equipped with radios and multicolored lights. He is currently working on a similar model for water skis.
Believe It!   Not!

b. A 16-passenger vehicle was created in 1827 by George Pocock. It was propelled by two huge kites flying from a single cord.
Believe It!   Not!

c. The Amphibian Marsh Buggy was a combination of car, tractor, and boat. With 10-foot-tall wheels, the buggy was used to navigate the Florida Everglades.
Believe It!   Not!

d. Robert Edison Fulton Jr. designed an airplane that could be converted into a car by removing its wings, propeller, and tail.
Believe It!   Not!

BONUS GAME

Get up and go! And while you're at it, connect these five modes of transportation to their "birthplace."

1. Motorcycle
2. Submarine
3. Roller skate
4. Snowmobile
5. Ambulance

a. New Hampshire, USA
b. France
c. Holland
d. Cannstadt, Germany
e. The Netherlands

All inventions start out with an idea. Sometimes the idea results from pure serendipity—other times it's the result of finding a problem that needs solving.

Fasten-ating Idea: Swiss scientist George de Mestral invented Velcro in the 1940s after studying burrs he found clinging to his clothing when he returned home from a walk through the fields.

Imagine That!

Which of these famous American inventors was kidnapped as a baby and ransomed for a horse?

a. Thomas Edison
b. George Washington Carver
c. Benjamin Franklin
d. Eli Whitney

The Right Touch: In 1829, Louis Braille, who was blind from birth, invented a way for the blind to read. He got the idea from French army troops, who punched marks in thick paper when sending messages so that they could "read" them in the dark trenches at night.

325

The *Real* Real McCoy: In the 1800s, inventor Elijah McCoy, the son of slaves, made a lubrication system that was so popular, buyers routinely inquired if they were getting "the real McCoy." To this day, when nothing else will do, people still insist on having "the real McCoy."

Crime Wave: In 1906, Lee De Forest invented a type of vacuum tube that greatly amplified weak radio signals. Unfortunately, before its true worth was realized, De Forest was arrested for selling stock in his invention, which was thought to be nothing but worthless glass.

Strong Suit: Having once survived an encounter with a grizzly bear, Troy Hurtubise invented a suit that is 50 times stronger and 85% lighter than steel so he could observe the big animals without putting himself in danger. To test it out, he stood in front of a brick wall while a car suspended on wires was swung into his chest like a pendulum. The 35,000-pound impact decimated the brick wall, yet left its wearer unharmed.

Keeping Current:

When his wife died in 1829, Samuel Morse was away from home at the time, and the news took a week to reach him. Grief-stricken, Morse, an artist, boarded a ship with the hope of finding some distraction in the art

galleries of Europe. On his return trip, he heard an American scientist lecture that "electric current is instantaneous." In college, Morse had learned that electricity is fluid. Perhaps, he reasoned, the current could be interrupted and clicks could be made by an electromagnet opening and closing the circuit—a short click for a dot and long one for a dash. If such a thing were possible, people would not have to wait weeks to get life-altering messages. Morse experimented with his idea for years and finally, in 1844, the first telegraph line was strung and the first message instantly communicated from Baltimore to Washington, D.C.

Imagine That!

In 1837, Thomas Davenport of Brandon, Vermont, patented America's first electric motor. He wound its magnet with silk from his . . .

a. top hat.
b. necktie.
c. wife's wedding dress.
d. own silkworms.

BEEP!

BEEP! BEEP!

BEEP! BEEP!

High-Tech Cattle Calls: In Japan, researchers have invented pagers for cows so that they can be beeped to come to the barn at milking time.

Just Spit It Out: Spitting out toothpaste could get very messy in a gravity-free environment, so a toothpaste that can be swallowed was invented especially for astronauts.

Painless Panes: You've heard of self-cleaning ovens. Now PPG Industries in Pittsburgh, Pennsylvania, has come up with a self-cleaning glass called SunClean.

SunClean glass is lined with a transparent coating that breaks down dirt and bird droppings in the sun. When it rains, the remaining residue washes away without streaking.

Imagine That!

The first full-length movie ever shown on TV was called *The Heart of New York.* It was about the invention of . . .

a. the skyscraper.
b. the subway.
c. the washing machine.
d. neon lights.

Out of the Mouths of Wasps: René Antoine Ferchault de Réaumur was walking through the woods in the early days of the 18th century when he passed a wasp's nest. When he examined it, he saw that it was made from a crude form of paper. He concluded that the wasps had digested tiny bits of wood to produce the paper. Thus the idea for the modern process of making paper from wood was born.

On the Ball: A company in Illinois has developed a baseball that displays the speed at which it is thrown.

Can Do: In 1999, a research company in London, England, developed a "smart" garbage can that is able to read bar codes and sort waste into separate recycling bins. The can also records which items the household has run out of and needs to replace.

Mini-bots: Sometimes the only way to get inside tight spaces is to dismantle them. Soon it may be possible to send in the Mini Autonomous Robot Vehicle Jr. (MARV Jr. for short) to do the job. The

size of a cherry and equipped with tanklike treads, MARV Jr. could crawl through pipes or between walls. Its builders at Sandia National Laboratories hope to add a radio so MARV Jr. robots can communicate with humans—and with one another, so that they can work in swarms, like insects.

Slugging It Out: The SlugBot is a lawn mower-sized machine with a long arm that shines red light on the ground to identify slugs. When it finds one, it picks it up and drops it in a storage bin. When the bin is full, the SlugBot heads for a processor equipped with bacteria that will gobble up the slugs and convert them into a natural gas. The gas is then put into a fuel cell that in turn powers the SlugBot—so it can go out and collect more slugs.

Cool Idea:

Sometimes brilliance lies in simplicity, as a low-tech invention by Nigerian teacher Mohammed Bah Abba has proved. His rural area has no electricity, so there are no refrigerators. With no safe way to preserve leftover food, it had to be thrown away. Bah Abba's invention has changed that.

One earthenware pot is placed inside a larger one and the space between them is filled with moist sand. The inner pot is filled with vegetables and the whole thing is covered with a wet cloth. As water in the sand evaporates through the surface of the outer pot, the heat in the inner pot is drawn out and carried away. The vegetables can last for three weeks or more. Bah Abba gave away 12,000 of his Pot-in-Pot Preservation/Cooling Systems. Later, he sold them for 40 cents each to help cover the cost of manufacturing.

In 2000, Bah Abba received a $75,000 Rolex Award for Enterprise, which he plans to use to expand his distribution throughout northern Nigeria.

Imagine That!

The hourglass was invented in order to limit the length of . . .

a. sermons.
b. hard-boiling eggs.
c. doctors' house calls.
d. chess moves.

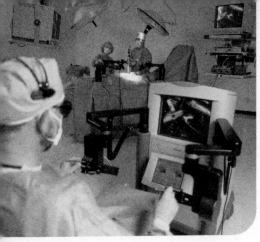

Remote-Control Surgery: Closed-chest heart surgery was developed by NASA for operating on astronauts in space. Here on Earth, surgeon Douglas Boyd operated on John Penner, a farmer who had suffered a heart attack but could not be away from his work for the three months he'd need to recover from conventional heart surgery. On October 6, 1999, in an operating room that looked like the site of a virtual-reality game, holes less than one-fourth of an inch wide were made in Penner's chest so three robotic arms could fit inside and perform the surgery. Dr. Boyd, sitting six feet away from his patient, guided the arms by remote control. The operation was a success, and the recovery period was so drastically reduced that Penner was back tending his cows in three days.

On the Beam:
A motorized wheelchair can be operated by eye movements, which interrupt a light beam when the user wears special glasses.

Imagine That!

In the 1600s, British naval officer Sir Kenelm Digby invented a salve that was supposed to heal a wound when applied to . . .

a. the weapon that caused it.
b. a picture of the king.
c. Sir Digby's mustache.
d. a scalpel.

Sounding It Out:

A robot guide for blind people designed in Japan emits ultrasound waves that bounce off obstacles. Then it will lead a blind person around them or, if it is not safe to proceed, wait until the obstacles disappear. It can even

plot the best route from start to finish. Unfortunately, it doesn't wag its tail or give its owner affection.

Toying with Baby:
California's Crump Institute for Medical Engineering has developed a breathing teddy bear that helps regulate a baby's sleep patterns while it monitors vital signs.

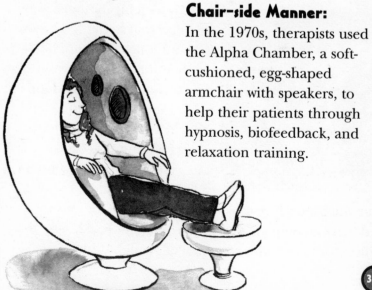

Chair-side Manner:

In the 1970s, therapists used the Alpha Chamber, a soft-cushioned, egg-shaped armchair with speakers, to help their patients through hypnosis, biofeedback, and relaxation training.

Stink-Free Shoes:

To combat smelly-feet syndrome, many companies are developing new lines of shoes, boots, and sandals that have been coated with AgION's silver-based antimicrobial compound. The fewer microbes floating around, the better your shoes are likely to smell.

All Hung Up: In 1903, when Albert J. Parkhouse arrived at his job at the Timberlake Wire and Novelty Company in Jackson, Michigan, there were no open coat hooks left. Without much thought, he reached for a piece of wire, bent it into two oblong hoops, twisted the ends together, and formed a hook in the middle. Then he hung his coat on it and went to work. The owners of the company liked the idea so much that they took out a patent on Parkhouse's idea. The company made a fortune, but Parkhouse, the inventor of the wire coat hanger, made nothing.

Wheeling and Dealing: In 1937, while watching his customers lug their groceries in handheld baskets up and down the aisles of his grocery store in Oklahoma City, Sylvan Goldman had what he thought was a brilliant idea: He invented the wheeled shopping cart and placed several in his store. But old habits die hard, and no one wanted to use them. It wasn't until he hired people to pretend they were shoppers and push the carts around the store that his idea finally started to catch on.

Imagine That!

Rows of buttons were first placed on shirtsleeves to . . .

a. prevent them from riding up beneath jacket sleeves.
b. keep people from wiping their noses on them.
c. help children learn how to count.
d. serve as decorations.

No Pressing Problems: Corpo Nove, a fashion company in Florence, Italy, has developed a fabric that needs no ironing. The Oricalco shirt is made of titanium-alloy fibers interwoven with nylon. No matter how wrinkled it gets, a few shots of air from a hair dryer will make the shirt look as if it came straight from the cleaners. The price tag? Four thousand dollars.

Avoiding Cat-astrophe: Englishman Percy Shaw was driving home one extremely dark and foggy night when he suddenly caught sight of a cat's eyes glowing in the dark. He stopped his car to avoid hitting the cat and realized that the cat had been sitting on a fence. Beyond the fence was a steep drop. If Shaw had not seen the cat first, he would have plunged over the cliff. That's when he got the idea for road reflectors—an idea that has since saved countless lives.

Imagine That!

Abul-Hassan, who in the 13th century, invented the hour by dividing the day into 24 equal parts, was . . .

a. an Indian novelist.
b. an Arabian poet.
c. an Egyptian engineer.
d. a Turkish mathematician.

Ripley's Believe It or Not! Brain Buster

What will they think of next? The following creations took a ton of imagination. But can you spot the one that is totally imaginary?

a. Just think! No more noisy, hard-to-start gas-powered lawn mowers. With Deanna Porath's combination tricycle and lawnmower, you can pedal around the yard, cutting the grass—while exercising at the same time.
Believe It!   Not!

b. Now you can hang art on your wall that will warm up the room at the same time. Gord Hamilton of Ontario, Canada, creates paintings that are embedded with hidden electric elements that act as heaters.
Believe It!   Not!

c. Jake & Jake Inc., a brother-in-law team from Maryland, crafted a must-have for the truly pampered pet. Their dog beds massage dogs' muscles, lulling tired pooches to sleep.
Believe It!   Not!

d. Checkers isn't just for two! A three-person checkerboard and a four-handed checkerboard were invented by Marion Hodges and Howard Wood respectively.
Believe It!   Not!

BONUS GAME

The following famous people made history. But can you match them up with their lesser-known creations?

1. Thomas Edison

2. Benjamin Franklin

3. Leonardo da Vinci

4. Thomas Jefferson

5. Sir Isaac Newton

a. A walking stick that converts into a stool

b. The harmonica

c. The wheelbarrow

d. Pet doors

e. Christmas tree lights

Here are some kid inventors who didn't give up until they found new ways to solve some old problems.

Wrist Warmers:

When the gap between 10-year-old Kathryn "K-K" Gregory's coat and mittens left her wrists cold and wet, she thought up Wristies. Not only have Wristies been a hit with kids but also with adults who work with their hands outside or in cold buildings, or who have arthritis, carpel tunnel syndrome, or circulation problems. K-K's invention has won her several awards as well as an appearance on *The Oprah Winfrey Show*.

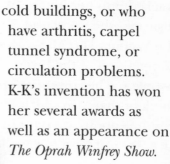

Imagine That!

When he was 11 years old, Antoine Vial of France invented a clothespin that alerted people that their laundry was dry by . . .

a. sounding a buzzer.
b. flashing a light.
c. turning blue.
d. dimming the house lights.

Cool Idea: One winter night in 1905, 11-year-old Frank Epperson stirred powdered soda pop mix into a jar of water and left it out on the porch of his San Francisco home. That night the temperature dropped, hitting a record low. When Frank went outside the next morning, he found that the mixture had frozen around the stirring stick. The next summer, he made "Epsicles" in the icebox and started selling them. This tasty treat is still being sold—only now it's called a Popsicle.

Clean Sweep: Twelve-year-old Jennifer Garcia's job was to vacuum and sweep the dirt that was constantly being tracked into her home. "Why not vacuum dirty shoes instead?" she wondered. That's when she got the idea for the Vacuum Dirt Mat—which won the New York State competition of the Invent America! contest. When people see her invention, they always say, "Why didn't I think of that?" To which Jennifer replies, "Sometimes the best inventions are right in front of us, staring us in the face. We just have to keep looking for them."

Big Deal:
In 1988, when she was 11 years old, Hannah Cannon of Hollywood, California, invented Cardz, a game that combined traditional playing cards with Scrabble. People in the toy business were so impressed with Hannah's game that she became the first child ever permitted on the floor of the International Toy Fair, the major annual toy-makers' convention.

Stub-Born: Some of Robbie Marcucci's favorite color crayons were too short to use. They would have gone to waste if he hadn't thought up the Crayon-Saver—an invention that works the same way a push-up pop does. Robbie's Crayon-Saver was such a hit that it won him the blue ribbon at his school's invention fair.

Imagine That!

At the age of four, John Parker of Vermont invented "ice star," a device that keeps . . .

a. ice cubes from sliding out of the glass while you're drinking.
b. shoes from slipping on ice.
c. ice-cream cones from dripping on your hands.
d. the blades of ice skates from getting dull.

On a Roll: Meredith Tucker loves to ice-skate and to in-line skate, too. So in 1997, at the age of 12, she invented Ice Blades, which utilizes a set of clip-on wheels to combine both skates in one. Now she doesn't have to waste time changing her skates when she zips home from the ice-skating rink in Shaker Heights, Ohio.

Noise Flash:
When he was eight years old, Brian Berlinski of Clifton, New Jersey, invented a silent car horn for the hearing-impaired—a light on the dashboard flashes at the sound of a honking horn.

Imagine That!

When they were eight and six years old, Sarah Cole Racine and her brother Brett invented edible tape to . . .

a. decorate food to make it more appetizing.
b. label food contents for finicky eaters.
c. personalize food portions so that everyone got an equal share.
d. make sloppy food easier to eat.

Handy Dipe and Wipe: When her baby brother needed changing, five-year-old Chelsea Lanmon of Texas fetched the powder, wipes, and diapers for her mother. If everything was packaged together, Chelsea figured she could save some time. So she sprinkled powder in a baby wipe, then folded it, and with her mother's help, sewed it up, and poked holes in it so that the powder would come out a little at a time. Next she made a pocket from the outside covering of one diaper and attached it to another one with double-edged tape. Chelsea won the national Invent America! competition for her invention, which she patented in 1994 at the age of eight.

Going Batty: In 1997, nine-year-old Austin Meggitt wanted to safely carry his bat and glove with him as he zipped around Amherst, Ohio, on his bike. His invention, the Glove and Battie Caddie, later won the Grand Prize in the Ultimate Invention contest sponsored by the Discovery Channel. In  1999, Austin was inducted into the National Gallery for America's Young Inventors at the National Inventors Hall of Fame.

343

Spotting Spot:

When he was six years old, Collin Hazen of North Dakota wanted a way to play ball with his dog on warm summer nights. The only trouble was that on a moonless night, it was hard to see

where the dog was. That's why Collin invented a battery-powered dog collar that glows in the dark.

Purr-fectly Edible:

Six-year-old Susan Goodin of Oklahoma loved her cats but hated washing the smelly food off the spoon when she fed them. When she heard about an invention contest, Susan had an idea. With some help from her grandmother, she came up with the Edible Cat Spoon, a garlic-flavored spoon that was strong enough to scoop the cat food from the can—and chewable as well. Now Susan just dumps the spoon in the bowl and her kitties get an extra treat. The cats are happy and so is Susan, who took first prize in the contest.

Imagine That!

In 1992, six-year-old James Jemtrud invented the Sucker Tucker for the purpose of . . .

a. keeping a baby's pacifier handy.
b. saving a straw to use again.
c. saving lollipops.
d. keeping a baby's bottle free of lint.

License to Win:

One day, ten-year-old Meghan Renee Hatfield was waiting with her mom in the checkout line at Kmart while the cashier copied her mother's license number onto the check. Meghan wondered why the cashier couldn't just stick the check in a slot and scan the license number into the cash register. Holding that thought, Meghan, who had twice entered the Invent America! contest but never won, decided to invent the Driver's License Number Scanner. As it turned out, three times was the charm. Meghan was the third-grade winner for the state of West Virginia.

No Fuss, No Muss:

A finalist in the 2001 Hammacher Schlemmer's Search for Invention competition, Carmina O'Connor of Illinois, has patented her Mashed Potato Machine, which cooks, mashes, and flavors potatoes in only 20 minutes. Just insert the potatoes, then add water and seasonings. The machine does the rest.

Dial-a-Meal:

What do you get when you combine a telephone, a phone flasher, an electric massager, and some fish food? A remote-control fish-feeder, of course. This invention was developed in the 1990s by nine-year-old Eric Bunnelle of Columbia, Missouri. What inspired him? His mother said he could only have a goldfish if he could figure out how to feed it while he was on vacation.

Going Squirrelly:

When Esther and Annemarie Hoffman of Euclid, Ohio, were ages 13 and 10, they invented a bird-feeder made of recycled plastic bottles that's totally squirrel-proof. Their first one was so successful that they've created a new and better model called The Transformer Bird Feeder. To market them, the girls (with a little help from their father) formed their own company, called Two Sisters and Their Dad.

Foul Ball!

Every fall, 11-year-old Lindsey Clement's Texas backyard is filled with spiky egg-shaped seedpods from 16 sweet gum trees. Besides being painful if stepped on, the seedpods are a pain to clean up. Lindsey decided to do something about it. She invented the Gumball Machine, which automatically picks up the seedpods and deposits them in a disposable bag. In 2000, her invention won her the Craftsman/NSTA Young Inventor Competition.

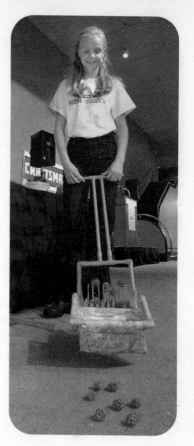

Imagine That!

When she was 11 years old, Melanie LaMontagne of Ontario, Canada, invented . . .

a. earmuffs for cats.
b. umbrellas for bird-feeders.
c. galoshes for guinea pigs.
d. snowshoes for dogs.

Tasty Fit: In 1992, when she was 11 years old, Elizabeth Anne Druback of New York invented a way to make visits to the dentist a little more enjoyable. She designed dental gloves called Flavor Fingers that come in root beer, coconut, and strawberry.

Long Reach:

Jeanie Low of Texas invented a foldaway Kiddie Stool when she was still in kindergarten. One day, Jeanie's step stool fell apart because people kept stumbling over it. Since she needed a stool to reach the bathroom sink, her mom took her shopping for a new one. When Jeanie couldn't find what she had in mind—a stool that would always be there but could also be kept out of the way—she decided to invent one. The stool she designed and built with her father's help attaches to the cabinet door under the sink and has hinges that allow it to fold. Jeanie patented the design in 1992, and now others can buy her Kiddie Stools either ready-made or in a kit to put together themselves.

Kids say the darndest things . . . *and* they make cool inventions! The items below are all about clever kids and their crazy creations. Are you clever enough to catch the one that's been created just for you?

a. A kindergartner got off on the right foot when she was inspired to create a gadget called the "Surefooter." The device helps kids make sure they have their shoes on the right feet.

Believe It!   **Not!**

b. Nine-year-old Jennifer "Spitster" Roy of Hicksville, New York, was bored with the usual distance-based watermelon seed-spitting contests. So she started a new game by crafting a device to measure the speed at which the seeds were spit.

Believe It!   **Not!**

c. In 1955, Ronald Rolfe and Edward Manchester (both 15) combined parts from an old buggy and some farm machinery to create a real working automobile.

Believe It!   **Not!**

d. At the age of ten, Becky Shroder of Toledo, Ohio, invented a luminescent way of writing in the dark.

Believe It!   **Not!**

BONUS GAME

These five crafty kids came up with some pretty cool ideas. Can you match each creation to the age of its inventor?

1. A water-conserving sprinkler system by Larry Villella

2. Earmuffs by Chester Greenwood

3. Dissolving golf tees by Casey Golden

4. Insect-repelling laundry detergent by Brittany Cormier

5. Glow-in-the-dark toilet seats by Clint Lenz

a. 13
b. 15
c. 12
d. 6
e. 10

POP QUIZ

One more round! You know all about the
Incredible Inventions in this book, right? Maybe
you're thinking, *I could've created some of them
myself.* Well then, strut your stuff by acing this pop
quiz. (With five points for every correct answer, it
will really boost your score, too!)

1. Which of the following *explosive* stories is true?
a. Pharmacist John Walker discovered matches when a
flammable glob of chemicals stuck to his stirring stick.
b. The idea for firecrackers came about when a woman
in 12th-century Malaysia accidentally ignited a barrel of
gunpowder.
c. Jonathan Reiss, an engineer who grew up alongside
an inactive volcano, invented a volcanic eruption
detector when he was 13.
d. "Eternal Flame Candles" were invented and sold by
Elvis fan Roslyn Gottlieb following the King's death in
1977. Some of the candles are still burning today.

2. Rubber is made from . . .
a. sand.
b. gum.
c. tree sap.
d. tree bark.

3. Three of the following toy stories are true. Can you tell which one is just playing with your mind?

a. The Slinky was invented by accident when Richard James tried to create a special spring for ship instruments.

b. Before getting its name, Silly Putty was used by circus clowns to make round red noses. It wasn't until 1943 that it was marketed as a toy.

c. Teddy bears were named for President Teddy Roosevelt after a particularly peaceful hunting trip.

d. Play-Doh was created by a man who was trying to come up with a new cleaning product.

4. Exploding golf balls that can be easily located were patented in 1990.

Believe It!   Not!

5. Which of the following mechanical animals has *not* been invented, according to the files of Robert Ripley?

a. Cat

b. Bird

c. Dog

d. Monkey

6. Phrenology is the study of . . .

a. animal fears.

b. sleeping habits.

c. interpersonal relationships.

d. the shape of people's skulls.

7. Which of the following did Thomas Edison *not* invent?

a. The cement house

b. A perpetual cigar

c. A voice-powered sewing machine

d. The radio

8. In 1896, a 17-foot long tricycle was built to hold 15 people.

Believe It!   Not!

9. World's weirdest water vehicles! Which one of these is *not* to be believed? (Because it's not real!)

a. Water-wave in-line skates

b. A floating tricycle

c. An underwater bicycle

d. A PowerSki Jetboard

10. "The Real McCoy" refers to the famous inventor . . .

a. Lynn McCoy.

b. Abraham McCoy.

c. Elijah McCoy.

d. June McCoy.

11. Which one of the following innovations is nothing but "pure invention"?

a. A boat driven by wasps

b. Self-cleaning glass

c. Cow pagers

d. A baseball that displays its speed

12. Samuel Morse was inspired to invent the telegraph because . . .

a. he wanted to keep in touch with cousins who lived 200 miles away.

b. he worked on a ship that spent weeks at sea.

c. he was out of town when his wife died, and it took a week for the news to reach him.

d. war plans could be more easily communicated.

13. Which of the following will the Mini Autonomous Robot Vehicle Jr. (MARV Jr.) *not* be capable of doing?

a. Working in teams

b. Communicating with humans

c. Crawling through pipes

d. Navigating the ocean floor

14. An eight-year-old boy invented a silent car horn for the hearing-impaired.

Believe It!   Not!

15. Which of the following creative creations was *not* a kid's brainchild?

a. Edible tape

b. Ice-cream sundaes

c. Popsicles

d. Glow-in-the-dark dog collars

Answer Key

Chapter 1

Accidentally Awesome!
Page 281: **b.** death.
Page 283: **b.** sheer stupidity.
Page 284: **a.** causing molecules in food to rub against each other.
Page 287: **d.** vanilla.
Page 289: **c.** Orthodontists use it to create dental molds.
Page 290: **b.** three billion pounds of potatoes.
Page 292: **d.** Life Savers
Page 294: **b.** soap.
Brain Buster: d. is false.
Bonus Game: 1=c; 2=d; 3=a; 4=b; 5=e

Chapter 2

No Way!
Page 297: **d.** lit a candle.
Page 299: **a.** mouse ears.
Page 301: **b.** snoring.
Page 303: **d.** last breath.
Page 305: **a.** a needle.
Page 306: **b.** famous people.
Page 308: **d.** jalapeño peppers.
Page 310: **d.** deicer on highways.
Brain Buster: c. is false.
Bonus Game: 1=a; 2=b; 3=e; 4=c; 5=d

Chapter 3

Way to Go!

Page 313:   **c.** a model of a horse's head in front.

Page 315:   **c.** filter car fumes.

Page 316:   **d.** Abraham Lincoln.

Page 319:   **c.** porcelainized bathtub.

Page 320:   **b.** an ever-saddled horse that eats nothing.

Page 322:   **a.** ammonia.

Brain Buster: a. is false.

Bonus Game: 1=d; 2=c; 3=e; 4=a; 5=b

Chapter 4

It Works!

Page 325:   **b.** George Washington Carver

Page 327:   **c.** wife's wedding dress.

Page 328:   **c.** the washing machine.

Page 331:   **a.** sermons.

Page 332:   **a.** the weapon that caused it.

Page 335:   **b.** keep people from wiping their noses on them.

Page 336:   **b.** an Arabian poet.

Brain Buster: c. is false.

Bonus Game: 1=e; 2=b; 3=c; 4=a; 5=d

Chapter 5

Kids Incorporated!

Page 339: **b.** flashing a light.

Page 341: **a.** ice cubes from sliding out of the glass while you're drinking.

Page 342: **d.** make sloppy food easier to eat.

Page 344: **c.** saving lollipops.

Page 347: **d.** snowshoes for dogs.

Page 348: **a.** LEGO toys

Brain Buster: b. is false.

Bonus Game: 1=c; 2=b; 3=a; 4=d; 5=e

Pop Quiz

1. **a.**
2. **c.**
3. **b.**
4. **Believe It!**
5. **b.**
6. **d.**
7. **d.**
8. **Not!**
9. **a.**
10. **c.**
11. **a.**
12. **c.**
13. **d.**
14. **Believe It!**
15. **b.**

What's Your Ripley's Rank?

Ripley's Scorecard

Well done! You've busted those brain cells over some of the world's most wacky gadgets and gizmos. Now it's time to tally up your answers and get your Ripley's rating. Are you just **Making a Start**? Or were you **Meant to Invent**? Add up your scores to find out!

Here's the scoring breakdown—give yourself:
★ **10 points** for every **Imagine That!** you answered correctly;

★ **20 points** for every fiction you spotted in the **Ripley's Brain Busters**;

★ **2** for every match you made on the **Bonus Games**;

★ and **5** for every **Pop Quiz** question you answered correctly.

Here's a tally sheet:
Number of **Imagine That**
questions answered correctly: _____ x 10 = _____
Number of **Ripley's Brain Buster**
fictions spotted: _____ x 20 = _____
Number of **Bonus Games**
matches made: _____ x 2 = _____
Number of **Pop Quiz** questions
answered correctly: _____ x 5 = _____

Total the right column for your final score: _____

0-100
Making a Start

Okay, so you're not exactly bursting with the creative power of invention. But you made it this far! And the amazing world of Ripley's is sucking you in . . . slowly. With some patience, you'll no doubt develop that weird and wacky Ripley's insight into separating fact from fiction. And once that starts, inventive behavior may be just around the corner!

101-250
Discovering Daily

The creative juices are flowing! You're really starting to get into all these extraordinary innovations. But you need to embrace your inner Ripley by brushing up on all of his bizarre factoids. Knowledge is power, my friend, and with a little more insight into the unusual, you'll be on your way to becoming a real Ripley's-style inventor.

251-400
Constantly Creating

Gadgets, gizmos, and wacky stuff is all you. You've certainly got the 411 on unbelievable inventions and discoveries—and you're not afraid to flaunt it. Separating fact from fiction like a pro, you almost reach the level of Robert Ripley himself. But of course, there's always more discovering to be done . . . .

401-575

Meant to Invent

Congratulations! You've reached the blissful state of Ripley's genius. In fact, maybe you know a little *too* much. All that bizarre info taking up space in your head—it may not be so healthy! You're both a gadget guru *and* a Ripley's groupie. Know what that means? It's time for you to invent something totally wacky yourself so that *you* can go down in Ripley's history.

Believe It!®

Photo Credits

281 X-ray/Worldwide rights, excluding countries that do not recognize U.S. copyright protection, courtesy of the American College of Radiology

282 Arthur Fry; 286 Patsy Sherman/3M

282 Safety Pins; 279, 301 Dimple-making Machine/ U.S. Patent and Trademark Office

288 Theodore Roosevelt Cartoon/Copyright Unknown

291 Ice-cream Sundaes; 293 Chocolate-chip Cookies/CORBIS

303 Thomas Edison/National Park Service/Edison National Historic Site

304 One-hand Clock/R. O. Schmitt Fine Arts

307 Max Factor/Proctor & Gamble Cosmetics/Noxell Corporation

310 Nikola Tesla/Tesla Wardenclyffe Project Archives

313 AUTOnomy Concept Car/2002 General Motors Corporation. Used with permission of GM Media Archives

314 Lunar Roving Vehicle/NASA

316 Edmund Halley/Royal Astronomical Society Library

317 PowerSki Jetboard/PowerSki International Corporation

318 SoloTrek™ XFV®/MJI

318 M400 Skycar/Moller International

321 Steve Roberts on BEHEMOTH/Nomadic Research Labs/www.microship.com

322 Rollerman/Christophe Lebedinsky

327 Samuel Morse/Evert A. Duyckinick Portrait Gallery of Eminent Men and Women in Europe and America. New York: Johnson, Wilson & Company, 1873

330 MARV Jr./Sandia National Laboratories

332 Remote-Control Surgery/Computer Motion, Inc.

334 Albert J. Parkhouse/Gary Mussell

339 Kathryn "K-K" Gregory wearing Wristies®/H. Scott Gregory, Jr.

343 Austin Meggitt/Anne Meggit

345 Mashed Potato Machine/Hammacher Schlemmer

346 Esther and Annemarie Hoffman/Dennis Hoffman/Two Sisters and Their Dad

347 Lindsey Clement/Craftsman/NSTA